IF I'M THE
BETTER PLAYER,
WHY CAN'T
I WIN?

IF I'M THE BETTER PLAYER, WHY CAN'T I WIN?

by ALLEN FOX
with Richard Evans

A Tennis Magazine Book

Published by
Tennis Magazine
A New York Times Company
495 Westport Avenue
Norwalk, Connecticut 06856

Trade book distribution
by Simon and Schuster
A Division of Gulf & Western Corporation
New York, New York 10020

First Printing
ISBN: 0-914178-28-8
Library of Congress: 79-63332
Manufactured in the United States of America

PREFACE

Those of us who play tennis at average levels are often unable to relate our efforts to the awesome power and precision of a Connors or a Borg. We sometimes wonder whether they play the same game we do and frequently feel that any comparison, however remote, is futile. This is not true. In any field of endeavor, you can never go wrong by studying and, if possible, copying the best.

Much of this book is comprised of anecdotes and incidents that have occurred on the pro tour. We have used the pros as examples for one simple reason— they do it best. Both mentally, which is especially pertinent here, and physically, they set the standards. Particularly in the psychological area, there is much that we can seek to emulate, for even if our bodies are never going to attain the suppleness and grace of a Nastase or the brute strength of a Vilas, our minds will always be receptive to training and discipline.

Obviously, there are limits, even on the mental level. A brilliant business brain or great intellectual capacity is no guarantee that we will be able to reproduce the clinical, unwavering concentration and will-to-win of a Chris Evert Lloyd. However, throughout this book we have tried to analyze precisely how the pros are able to function at their lofty level and take from them that which will be of greatest use to you.

Although the setting for this study is the tennis court, performers in any competitive occupation should be able to derive some benefit from it. It is not necessary to play tennis to come face to face with such common psychological problems as defensiveness or the fear of losing. It is hoped, therefore, that the conclusions Allen Fox has drawn will be of as much use to the actress testing for a part or the businessman struggling to close a tough deal as they will be to the tennis player facing match point.

A word or two here about Fox. Allen is uniquely qualified to write this book. For the past several years, he has coached the Pepperdine University tennis team and has advanced their standing to the No. 5-ranked position in the United States. But no other doctor of psychology can match his record as a top tennis player. Ranked five times in America's Top 10, he played on the U.S. Davis Cup team three times and won the National Intercollegiate and National Hardcourt singles and the Canadian National title, among numerous other successes on the international circuit.

Nothing, however, quite matched his performance at the Pacific Southwest Championships in 1966. Before a succession of disbelieving crowds at the Los Angeles Tennis Club, Fox defeated Manuel Santana, Tony Roche, Fred Stolle and Roy Emerson in consecutive rounds. In doing so, Allen created a record for himself that may never be equalled, for those four great players were, at the time he beat them, the current holders of the world's four major titles. In the previous 12 months, Santana had won Wimbledon, Roche the French, Stolle Forest Hills and Emerson the Australian title. So, in effect, Allen had created his own personal version of the Grand Slam. To have beaten all four in one tournament was, of course, an amazing achievement, but almost as amazing was the fact that he had the opportunity to do it. Normally, his opponents would have been seeded Nos. 1 through 4 and two of them would, therefore, have met in the semifinal. However, Dennis Ralston, a finalist that year at Wimbledon and a local California star, had been given the No. 4 spot in the seeding, thus giving Allen the chance of meeting in succession the winners of all four Grand Slam events.

I imagine that it has always been a great deal more fun playing with Allen Fox than against him, for, as the reader will quickly discover, he is a tough competitor who believes that there is no substitute for winning. As it has been my good fortune to work alongside him at a typewriter rather than to play against him across a net, I have had the better end of the deal—enjoying not only his hospitality in Santa Monica during the five months that it took to write this book, but also the satisfaction of working with a first-class mind. For me, personally, it was a stimulating and rewarding experience and I feel sure you will find it equally so.

—Richard Evans

CONTENTS

CHAPTER 1.
DO YOU REALLY
WANT TO WIN?

TENNIS IS A GAME OF LIFE

A tennis match is a violent psychological struggle. Both antagonists are fighting for their own egos, seeking ways to strengthen their senses of power and enhance their self-images.

Does this sound a little overblown? After all, a tennis match is just a game. But what is a game other than a contest of sorts, played to obtain strictly psychological currency? Certainly, it is to be distinguished from "real" contests where more vital interests are at stake, such as food, shelter, security and other things necessary for the preservation of life.

But, let's take your job. You would probably not question that it is a matter of utmost seriousness. Earning a living as a banker, lawyer, auto salesman or builder is considered inconceivably more substantial than winning tennis matches—than playing "games." But how necessary is your particular job to maintaining life? Not very, in the United States. We are incredibly affluent and have many wants, but very few needs. If you lost your job, you would survive. Although you might feel disgraced and might not retain your former position psychologically, or your former "status" in the community, you would still eat, sleep and survive adequately.

For most of us, the game of life we play has little to do with survival and a great deal to do with seeing how much of America's excess wealth we can accumulate. Not because we really need it, but because acquiring a good slice of the pie boosts our self-image, increases our feelings of security and satisfies our need for achievement. Moreover, wealth and possessions are the way we keep score in business. That is how we know who is winning.

In other words, the game we play at the office includes most of the same psychological needs as the game we play on the tennis court. But one is called a game, the other work. By likening our professional and working lives to games, I am not belittling them; I am merely trying to put them in perspective, for both are based on our psychological as well as material needs.

Between 1968 and 1975, I worked in the investment business and during that time, I became aware of the similarities that exist between the covert warfare that takes place on a tennis court and the marginally less covert attrition that takes place during a business deal.

Over martini lunches, I used to hear a lot of talk about business etiquette. The man trying to sell me a deal usually stressed his moral commitment to long-term business relationships; and how I might be better off giving up certain points in the short term to enhance the relationships for the long term.

Although valid to an extent, this was often just so much sugar coating on the pie. I had to be aware of the possibility that he was after as large a slice of the pie as he could lay his hands on—right then and there. Underneath all the friendly talk, business is extremely rough and anyone who falls for the facade doesn't survive long.

In tennis, as in all games, there is a social facade based on rules and etiquette that attempts to shield both the viewer and the competitor from the harsher

14

elements of the combat. The need to win in a nice gentlemanly fashion is instilled into us very early. But beneath that clean, white veneer, a tennis match has all the potential required to become nasty, threatening and rough. This is true because, deep down, we all want to win no matter how reluctant we are to admit it to ourselves or to others. And if it is necessary to become nasty on court in order to win, many people will get nasty.

No matter what kind of genteel attitude your opponent may display, you don't really know what he is like until it gets down to the crunch. He may want to win very badly. Don't allow yourself to get so caught up in the etiquette of the game that you forget about winning.

The need to win in a nice gentlemanly fashion is instilled into us very early. But beneath that clean, white veneer, a tennis match has all the potential to become nasty, threatening and rough.

ARE YOU COMPETITIVE?

Fortunately or not, winning is tremendously important in our society. From earliest childhood, the concept is pounded into our unconscious in a multitude of subtle ways. We are often totally unaware that this conditioning has taken place and that we are, in fact, passing it onto our children and friends.

More so than in many other parts of the world, our American culture is goal-orientated and competitive because of the aggressive, risk-taking nature of the immigrant, going back to even the earliest colonists. The United States is, by definition, the land of opportunity. It was founded by people who wanted to better themselves and were prepared not only to work, but often to risk everything they owned, to achieve that betterment. But there are more people than "good things" in this life and to get our share, we are forced to compete. There are simply not enough houses in Beverly Hills to go round.

As a result, we have been raised on all manner of competitive score-keeping devices: school grades, children's games, athletic contests, even beauty pageants. All instill the competitive urge and make us aware of the benefits of ending up a winner. Often, we have parents who drive us on, urging us to win and sometimes punishing us if we do not.

You may say, "My parents weren't pushy . . . they didn't scold or press me if I didn't get all A's in school or win all my football games." But try as they might, your parents could not help but be happier when your report card showed an A rather than a C. Their praise was always stronger when you won rather than lost. Their joy was more real. They could not help it nor hide it. Neither could your teammates or friends. And you could not help but feel it in a thousand ways and incorporate it into your deepest fiber.

Children are not so dense that they cannot read between the lines—no matter what anyone says—and understand that they get more for winning and excellence than they do for losing and mediocrity. Moreover, this conditioning process does not end with childhood. It continues throughout our adult lives and lasts until the day we die. This is one reason why winning is so important to us—a subject we will discuss in detail in the following chapter.

BUILDING DEFENSES AGAINST LOSING
The average person soon discovers that he cannot win as often as he would like. Most people are doomed to lose often, because there are always more competitors than winners. Since the need to win is powerful, so also is the pain of loss. How then does the average person cope with the constant pain of loss? He employs defense mechanisms. In his conscious mind, he changes goals and convinces himself that winning is not his objective.

Sigmund Freud, who originated the concept, said that our egos (or that part of our psyches from which self-esteem is derived) must be protected from thoughts and realities that may be too painful for us to accept and deal with. There are many types of defense mechanisms, but they all serve the same purpose—the protection of the ego. And they all employ the same means—self-delusion and distortion of reality.

16

Fear of inadequacy is a constant companion in our lives, as is the nagging thought that we may be unable to accomplish the goals we have set for ourselves.

On the tennis court, the fact that we very much want to win but are unable to may be shameful to us.

On the tennis court, the fact that we very much want to win but are unable to may be shameful to us. The ego is at stake and we hurriedly build barriers to protect it. By using the defense mechanisms of repression and rationalization, we can shield our egos from facts which are incompatible with our feelings of self-esteem. We force them out of our conscious minds and replace them with a smoke screen of seemingly reasonable alternatives. Defensive players often cloak their desires to win by rationalizing, or explaining away, for example, that winning is less important than good sportsmanship, exercise, comraderie or just a good suntan. They are not simply saying this for the benefit of members of the club; they believe it—because they have to.

Defensive players don't compete with the vigor of real winners. Nor do they believe they want to. Just as an animal can be conditioned to avoid crossing a grid by electric shock, so can a person be conditioned to stop competing by the pain of loss.

For example, I have noticed my own defense mechanisms growing as my physical powers falter as I get older. When I was in my 20's, I competed fully every time I walked out on court. I would push the accelerator to the floor and something would always happen. I was constantly testing myself. This was enjoyable, despite many disappointments, because I usually won. Now, in my late 30's, I find myself physically unable to respond to the accelerator. I push it to the floor and often nothing happens. I have found myself more and more unwilling to compete 100 percent. If I start to get tired I wonder, "Why should I kill myself?" If I split sets with my opponent, I'm often quite willing to quit and call it a draw. Before, I used to invariably press for a decision.

The ability to maintain his competitive edge and hunger for victory after years of play on the tournament circuit is possibly the most amazing aspect of Ken Rosewall's seemingly interminable career at the top. Of course, he is also something of a physical phenomenon in his mid-40's to be able to last through long matches against powerful, young players. But that, in my opinion, is not so remarkable as his unceasing desire to compete and the willingness to expose himself to an increasing number of painful losses.

Making excuses. The vast majority of us cannot face the kind of pain Rosewall faces on a routine, voluntary basis. To protect ourselves, we erect numerous defensive walls that vary in size and texture. One of the most common is excuse-making, a type of rationalizing.

"It's too windy."

"The lights are so bad, I can't see the ball."

"The court is so slippery, I can't stand up."

"He gave me a bad call and if he wants the match that bad, let him have it."

"My arm hurts."

These are typical examples. We have all heard plenty more. There is usually some validity to all of them, but insecurity magnifies each negative factor out of all proportion. The test for whether defensive behavior is occurring is how realistic and practical the behavior is overall, not whether the excuse itself has some validity. When a player gets a bad call, all it costs him is one point. It is his reaction to it that can cost him the match.

Why should any rational person throw a match because he is angry over one bad call? Surely, it would be more reasonable to increase his efforts to win to teach the cheater a lesson. But he blows the match because he is insecure and fears that even if he redoubles his efforts, he might still lose. That would be too painful to accept, so he hides this knowledge from himself and backs off from the whole situation.

I exhibited a nasty illustration of defensive excuse-making one year at the U.S. Championships at

18

Forest Hills. I had reached the round of 16 and was scheduled to play Whitney Reed, a tough, but not great, player who had upset Chuck McKinley, the No. 1 American, in the previous round. If I beat Whitney, I would have been scheduled to play Rafael Osuna, whom I had defeated several times that year. It was a wonderful chance to reach the semifinal.

But I had been playing tournaments every week for five months and my nerves were starting to fray. The pressure was building. Although I didn't know it at the time, I couldn't take it.

The night before the match, my wife, Carol, and I got into a huge argument (the subject of which escapes me now). Still seething, I went on court the next day in a troubled frame of mind. I lost a close first set to Reed, but thoughts of how Carol had upset me kept flitting through my head. By the second set, I was furiously hitting balls as hard as I could to teach Carol a lesson. The legacy of our argument, I thought, had ruined my concentration and filled my mind with absurd logic. "The bitch," I said to myself, "has cost me Forest Hills," and I continued to take wild cuts at the ball.

Of course, I lost, but it took me a long time to realize that my own inability to handle the pressure was the real reason for my petulance. Carol was simply the nearest convenient target. We did have an argument, but I chose to build it into the massive trauma that eventually wrecked any chance I had of winning the match.

The inability to finish off a match. Eddie Edwards, an All-American and the top player on the Pepperdine University team in 1978–79, used to fall prey to a common variation of defensiveness. He used to have tremendous difficulty in finishing off matches after he had won the first set and had established a commanding lead in the second.

The first time he frittered away a big lead after I began coaching, I confronted him when he came off court and said, "What happened?"

19

Winning the last few points against a tough opponent is often a tense and unpleasant task. And, as with most nasty jobs, people tend to avoid them as long as possible.

"I just got overconfident," he replied. "I thought I had the match in the bag so I relaxed and stopped concentrating."

I looked at him for a second and said, "That's not what happened at all. In fact, you just didn't want to get down to the dirty business of finishing off the match."

As a match nears its end, the pressure mounts. Winning the last few points against a tough opponent is often a tense and unpleasant task. And, as with most nasty jobs, people tend to avoid them as long as possible. That was the case with Eddie. His insecurity, coupled with the desire to put off facing the pressure, made him convince himself he had plenty of leeway. Once convinced, he could take a breather and relax instead of getting down to business. I'll explain this in more detail in Chapter 6.

Most important, his good self-image could be maintained. It is no disgrace to lose because you are overconfident. Some players almost boast about it, recounting in the locker room afterward how they could have beaten the guy a dozen different ways but just got bored with it all. After all, loss of concentration seems to indicate that you could have won had you just chosen to concentrate. But being unable to finish off your opponent when you have him down is something else. That is considered a disgrace and no one likes to face it.

Since Edwards had gotten into trouble many times this way in the past and since he knew, logically, that his opponent was quite capable of coming back, it was clear that some type of self-delusion was operating. He had convinced himself that it was overconfidence and lack of concentration. But once those old masks were stripped away, the real problems—insecurity and fear—revealed themselves.

Mental distractions. There are other varieties of defensiveness which also involve concentration. In 1966, I was on tour in Australia with Charlie Pasarell,

20

who was ranked No. 1 in the United States the following year. He had reached the quarterfinals in Adelaide
and was playing Barry Phillips-Moore who was a clay-
court specialist—something of a rarity among Australian players. Fortunately for Pasarell, they were playing on grass which suited his big serve-and-volley
game perfectly. However, even during his years at the
top, Pasarell had a problem—he thought too much.

With Pasarell misfiring frequently, the match
turned into a marathon and he found himself serving
to save it at 5–6 in the fifth set. At 15–30, he thumped in
a big serve and followed it to the net. The return
floated invitingly to his big forehand volley, his favorite shot.

Later, Pasarell told me that just as he was about to
hit the volley, a perverse thought crossed his mind,
"What if I miss this?" That's all it took. The volley
smacked into the net, Phillips-Moore hit the next return for a winner and the match was over.

Pasarell had no business allowing errant thoughts
to creep into his mind during vital moments of play. It
was total lack of discipline on his part. At this stage of a
match, in particular, the mind must remain clear. But
with the frightful prospect of losing to a lesser player
—and a clay-court specialist at that—Pasarell's
defense mechanisms were triggered. The prospect
was too much for him and he found an out: lack of
concentration.

By allowing his concentration to lapse—in fact,
almost willing it to lapse—Pasarell had set the stage
for a mental escape. He removed his mind and conscious efforts from a situation that was becoming increasingly stressful. He refused to take the risk that he
could be beaten heads up by Phillips-Moore. Afterward, lack of concentration provided a handy excuse
for the loss. In fact, it was a real excuse, but only
because he had unconsciously manufactured it.

It is not always easy to see through the masquer-
ade of human behavior. Defensive thinking is so insid-
ious that the masks fit snugly onto our illusions, mak-

21

Real competition requires intense and prolonged concentration. If you blot out a substantial portion of your drive, you will lose much of your competitive effectiveness.

ing the whole costume seem eminently plausible. It is so easy and really quite believable to blame the lights when you can't see well, or your wife when she argues with you, or to substitute lack of concentration for fear of losing. But it is simply not reality.

The greater the defensiveness, the more your will to win is obscured. It becomes something different, such as the desire to be a good sport, or to get some exercise, or to feel good hitting the ball. In any case, it is of no further use to you in winning tennis matches. It is lost. Real competition requires intense and prolonged concentration. If you blot out a substantial portion of your drive, you will lose much of your competitive effectiveness.

ACCEPT THAT YOU *DO* WANT TO WIN

Because our needs to achieve and win are present in us at such a basic level, denying their existence, making excuses and setting up other defense mechanisms against them can cause more problems than they solve. Claiming and consciously believing that you do not want to win is simply denying a reality that exists in our society. You *do* want to win. You are kidding yourself and cheating yourself if you do not realize it.

When you deny your need to win, you make yourself a poor competitor and ultimately cause yourself to lose. When it is 5–all in the third set and both players are tired and thirsty, who is more likely to win . . . the player who believes he is playing for exercise or the player who openly acknowledges that he wants to win and knows he will be unhappy if he loses?

The tournament player, even if he is not a professional, openly and full-bloodedly competes. He possesses certain traits which we'll discuss in the next two chapters that make him a healthy competitor. His defense mechanisms are not up; if he loses he is miserable. Eventually, he learns to handle this; but immediately after the loss, he still hurts. The average player, on the other hand, may feel equally happy—win or lose. He has protected himself. A good way to test the

22

strength of your own defense mechanisms is to note your reactions to a loss . . . if you feel no pain or disappointment, your defense mechanisms have been active . . . if you have fully and openly competed, you will feel pain after losing.

The player whose defense mechanisms are powerful lives in a gray, paradoxical world. He feels neither great pain from loss nor great pleasure from victory. His inability to compete fully causes him to lose often and the losses, in turn, increase and reinforce the strength of his defense mechanisms. He feels vaguely uncomfortable with his "loser" psychology, but he does not know how to go about reversing it. He may even be afraid to look too deeply into this subject lest he disturb a lifetime of carefully constructed defenses and be forced to face the naked truth . . . that he wants to win but may be unable to do so.

I am not saying that you must compete with blind ferocity in every match or in all competitive situations. That would be excessive and exhausting. Rather, it is important that you acknowledge and understand your own competitive drives and the forces that keep them in check. Decide what your goals and desires really are; understand and confront your fears. For only with this understanding will you have control over yourself and your mental attitudes. Without it, you are subject to the ebbs and flows of outside forces. So strip away the mask and remember the wisdom of Shakespeare's Cassius when he said,

> "The fault, dear Brutus, is not in our stars
> But in ourselves, that we are underlings."

CHAPTER 2.
WHAT IT TAKES
TO BE A WINNER

Few athletes have put their hunger for success and their single-minded drive for victory on the line as brazenly and as consistently as Jimmy Connors. He wants to be a winner, and he wants the world to know it. At a very early age, Connors learned how to win. Learning how to lose took him a great deal longer.

Despite deep insecurities in his makeup, on court Connors exudes confidence. And by the very style of his game, he epitomizes drive. Confidence and drive—these are the factors that make Connors a winner. Without them, he would be like so many other talented players on the pro tour—a frequent loser whose natural ability enables him to win only once in a while. To become a true champion in any competitive endeavor, confidence and drive are absolutely essential.

Connors is an excellent model for any discussion about winning because these twin assets radiate from him. Each gesture, each shot, each expression signals confidence and drive as clearly as a lighthouse beacon.

There was no better demonstration of this than Connors' epic battle against Adriano Panatta in the 1978 U.S. Open at Flushing Meadow. If Connors had not been carrying a mighty storehouse of confidence

24

and drive, he would have lost that match. It was not simply that Panatta, a powerful and talented player, was playing well, but that whenever Connors thought he had finally got the match under control, the Italian tore the initiative out of his hands.

To become a true champion in any competitive endeavor, confidence and drive are absolutely essential.

Connors had weathered an amazing opening burst when Panatta had seemed virtually invincible and had fought back to lead by two sets to one. By winning the third set 6–1, Connors had established the kind of dominance that usually brings him a quick and decisive victory.

But Panatta charged back to take the fourth set, also by 6–1, and break for a 3–1 lead in the fifth. Again Connors weathered that onslaught to break Panatta in the sixth game to level at 3–3. But no sooner had he got the match back on an even keel than Panatta snatched his serve away to love in the very next game. For most players, that would have been the final psychological crusher. There is nothing more mentally debilitating than trying to climb a mountain when you are taking one pace forward and sliding two paces back. In a sense, that was what was happening to Connors but, unlike most of us, he wasn't dispirited. On the contrary, he was relishing every second of the fight. Every good shot he hit was used as a psychological booster to pump extra reserves of confidence and drive into his system.

Slapping his thigh, grunting with effort, hunching his shoulders and strutting back to the baseline after every winning shot—with every gesture Connors was telling the huge stadium court crowd, "Look at me. This is Jimmy Connors at work, doing what I do best. I have a worthy opponent and no matter what, I'm going to beat him."

There was no logic to that attitude. When Panatta collected new balls to serve for the match at 5–4, the odds were in favor of him doing the beating. But confidence and logic make poor bedfellows. Panatta was quickly reminded of that as Connors pulled off a series of superb service returns to break back for 5–5 and then hit one unbelievable single-handed back-hand on the run in the 12th game which helped him break the Italian's serve a second time—and clinch an incredible victory.

WHAT IS CONFIDENCE?

Confidence played a major part in enabling Connors to pull off that remarkable triumph. But what is confidence and what causes it? Basically, it is the expectation of success and, like any expectation, it is dependent on past experience. It is not, therefore, something that is inborn. It is learned and cumulative, depending upon the unique pattern of each person's success experience.

It is a conditioning process and, as such, is unconscious and sometimes illogical. For instance, if someone asks you whether or not the sun will come up tomorrow morning, you would tell him with total confidence that it will. Why? Because in the past it *always* has. If, every once in a while, it missed, you would not be so absolutely sure.

On a less obvious level, a small child might be climbing a tree and his father will say, "Jump! I'll catch you." The first time that happens the child might need a lot of persuading to overcome his fear. But, providing the father does not drop him, the child will need less persuasion the second time and possibly none at all the third. On the basis of past experience, he will have developed sufficient confidence to believe implicitly that his father will not drop him and therefore he will not hurt himself. Of course, it is possible that the father could make a mistake. But that does not concern the child, because he has no experience of it. Confidence illogically goes deeper than a strict assessment of the possibilities. It is an unconscious belief in the repetition of one's own past experience.

Winning and confidence are interdependent. For the tennis player, this reasoning yields a very important axiom: Confidence depends on winning just as winning depends on confidence. The more you win, the more you expect to win, hence the easier winning becomes. That may sound like circular reasoning. But all it means is that, to have the confidence to win, you must have built up a backlog of victories.

Where does the chain start? It starts very early in a player's career. Those players who make it to the top are usually those who were the best juniors in their particular area of the country. Even if they were not the best athletes around, they would certainly have had high athletic capability. This alone would have earned them more than their fair share of victories. But, in addition, and even more important, they would have been highly motivated and driven individuals. Combined with physical ability, this combination would lead to still more victories. As a result, the players would become accustomed to winning and so the seeds of confidence would be sown.

The winning-confidence-winning syndrome can be placed into two basic categories: 1) a massive backlog of victories acquired throughout a player's young life which would provide an overall umbrella of confidence; 2) recent victories which would account for the hot streaks that so many players enjoy from time to time.

Parents, in particular, should take careful note of the point I am making here. It is a common fallacy that your child should play the very best competition every day on the theory that "you only improve in tennis by playing someone better than yourself." Certainly, it is good, on occasion, to take the opportunity of playing against a top-class performer. Who would not seize the chance of getting on court with Arthur Ashe or Stan Smith if either happened to be passing through and in need of a hit?

But, if you have a promising 14-year-old who hits the ball well and is good enough to give a better player serious practice, it would be a mistake to have him play every day with the 17-year-old U.S. junior champion who just happened to live down the street. Every

> **Confidence depends on winning just as winning depends on confidence. The more you win, the more you expect to win, hence the easier winning becomes.**

day your son would get beaten. His strokes might improve, but victory would always remain beyond his grasp. Whenever he came close to winning, the older boy would be able to call on his superior experience and firepower to snatch the match away. Subconsciously, your teenager would start to develop a loser's mentality. Deep down, he would begin to feel that as soon as the match got tight, it would start to slip away from him.

Later on, he would carry that expectation of loss into tournaments. As a result of past defeats suffered whenever it got close, he would anticipate his opponent wiggling out of the tight corner once again and beating him. In other words, he would lose simply because he never learned how to win.

Confidence lies at the root of this problem. Confidence blossoms from the tree of success. It blossoms naturally, unthinkingly. It does not stop to query the quality of that success or even the manner of it. If you are a genuinely good player and crush all opposition early in your career, you will become a very confident tennis player. When you start playing at the senior level, it will not matter that your opponents are suddenly players of equal skill and of far greater experience. You will still have this gut feeling that if you push down hard on the accelerator at the crucial moments, you will win. For a time, at least, confidence alone will carry you through.

Billy Martin is a good example of this. He was totally dominant as a young player, winning every conceivable local and national junior title. He was a ferocious competitor and did a great job of hiding the inadequacies in his game behind a facade of superior confidence and a proven ability to guts it out and win.

The fact that he has structured and somewhat inflexible strokes, bad hands and not enough speed about the court did not catch up with him until two or three years after he joined the pro tour. For some time, good performances in the early rounds kept his ranking up in the 50's and 60's on the ATP computer.

However, slowly but surely the memory of title-winning success started to fade. Instead of expecting to win every time he walked on court, Martin began to learn what it was like to lose. He lost a little, then more, and finally quite a lot. Just as surely as winning had become a habit to him in his junior days, losing was becoming a habit as a pro. But it only happened because he was not yet showing the capacity to improve as a player. In the first couple of years, confidence alone allowed him to win more matches than his actual talent and game warranted.

THE DRIVE TO WIN

Of course, confidence alone will get you nowhere. Apart from a certain level of athletic ability, the other major quality you need to succeed on a tennis court is drive. No one has ever become a champion in any sport without possessing a high degree of drive. That surging compulsion for success which propels you forward through barriers of pain and effort to achieve your goal is indispensable to the winner. Some champions, like Connors, are so imbued with it that they appear to be forever tilted forward into the wind, fighting friend and foe alike in their all-consuming drive toward the mountain top.

Others—a rare breed of which Evonne Goolagong is a good example—appear so easygoing and casual as to possess no drive at all. But that is an illusion. No one wins Wimbledon without drive.

This quality we call drive can be analyzed as coming from several sources. First, there is the inborn drive that manifests itself in the need to attain competence or fulfillment. Second, there is the urge to obtain power or dominance. And, finally, there is the need for achievement, a drive which is learned in a child's early years and is goal-orientated and based on a system of rewards.

What motivates behavior. Two eminent American psychologists, R.W. White and Carl Rogers, have done the major work on what are termed "competence" and "self-actualization." Like so many other learned minds in their field, these psychologists have taken a certain aspect of personality and made it the cornerstone of their theories. Try to avoid the tendency to be confused by the apparent differences that may arise from these theories. To some degree they are all correct; all have a valid statement to make. No one, after all, can describe in a few succinct sentences such a complex and many-faceted subject as the human personality. And here, for clarity, we are oversimplifying the theories.

With this in mind, let us examine the prime components of drive. White maintains that human beings are motivated to achieve "competence" for its own sake rather than to satisfy some physiological need. Prior to this, the "party line" in psychology spearheaded by Freud was that all behavior ultimately came from the urge to get rid of unpleasant physiological deficits. The child's cry when he is hungry is an example.

But how do the deficit psychologists explain a child's need for love? That doesn't appear to be a physiological deficit. It is explained as a learned need. The child early on is totally dependent on his parents for satisfying all of his physical needs. He learns to associate his parents' physical warmth and love with these satisfactions. Later, there will be no memory of the connection, and the child will seek love for its own sake.

White, however, maintains that a baby often cries simply to make a noise, to test his vocal chords and not necessarily because he is hungry or demanding attention. This instinctive tendency extends to the whole field of play behavior. The way in which a small child experiments with his own body and manipulates objects in his playpen is all part of the first faltering steps in his search for competence—the striving to express, develop and control his capacities.

Rogers' theory is similar to White's but wider in

scope. Rogers calls his drive "self-actualization" and uses the term to describe man's inherent urge to use his biological abilities, believing that it is natural for us to test these abilities to their fullest. As with White's theory, self-actualization has no incentive other than an instinctive desire to do what we are able to do to the best of our ability.

Inevitably, some people self-actualize better than others. Within his own guidelines, Rogers places us all into two main categories: one in which the self-actualizing tendency is vigorously expressed, leading to the enhancement and enrichment of living, and the other in which the actualizing tendency is protectively and defensively expressed, leading to the mere maintenance of living.

People who self-actualize fully tend to live their lives fully. They are, to quote Rogers, "more open to feelings of fear and discouragement and pain as well as feelings of courage, tenderness and awe." They are, in other words, laying themselves on the line, opening themselves up to all of life's experiences and emotions, ready to meet with Kipling's twin imposters of triumph and disaster.

This, of course, is Connors personified. In the final minutes of that match against Panatta, Connors was self-actualizing himself out of his skin. In front of 18,000 people on a brand new stadium court at Flushing Meadow, Connors was living life at a peak of adrenaline-pumping excitement that few of us ever attain. Puffing up his chest when he hit a great shot, shaking his head in fury when he missed, Connors was laying his emotions and ambitions bare to an extent that stretches Rogers' idea of what he calls "a fully functioning person" to its limits.

As we shall see, other forces also drive Connors. But in that particular match, he was not playing for the money or the ultimate accolades of glory. He was merely reveling in the sheer joy of matching his ability blow for blow against the other guy, of relishing and basking in the unfolding of his talent. The gleeful joy

People who self-actualize fully tend to live their lives fully. This, of course, is Connors personified.

he revealed whenever he hit a good shot was almost childlike in its simplicity. And, indeed, the White/ Rogers theories embrace this aspect, for they maintain that we do what we are biologically capable of doing and that doing it well simply makes us feel good.

Sexual frustration. Freud had other ideas. The father figure of psychology, whose views on this particular subject seem almost passé now, would have led us into the bedchamber in search of answers. He would doubtlessly have maintained that the physical drives of the successful tennis stars are those of people with high sexual drives who are unable to find the obvious and normal outlet for that energy.

Even today, when everybody on the pro circuit is taking his job far more seriously, I would say that Freud's theory is flattened by the facts. Not only are the opportunities for sexual pursuits nearly always numerous at tournaments around the world, but the great majority of players seize those opportunities with relish. If Freud had been able to observe the performance of a few of the players both on court *and* in bed, he would have been forced to take his theories back to the drawing board in bewilderment (and, possibly, admiration!).

How inferiority feelings play a role. Alfred Adler, an Austrian breakaway member of Freud's original inner circle, seems to be nearer the mark for our purposes. Repudiating Freud's sexual theories, Adler maintained that people act to gain power, and that our desire for power stems from our need to compensate for feelings of inferiority. It was Adler who coined the phrase "inferiority complex" and theorized that we spend our lives struggling upward to achieve goals which will convince us of our self-worth.

Whether we are born with these feelings or whether we develop them very early in life, nobody knows. But it is clear that we have every opportunity to acquire feelings of inferiority from day one. From

32

the moment we are born, we are learning everything from people who can do everything better than we can. They—usually our parents—are bigger, stronger and more capable. They control us physically. If they will it, they can stop feeding us. Throughout all those early formative years, they hold the power of life and death over us. How can one help but feel inferior?

The competition that exists between human beings forms an intrinsic and absolutely indispensable part of our quest for success.

The release from that feeling begins when we start developing some power of our own—whether it be in school as a team leader or later in life as an army sergeant, a junior executive or a champion athlete. Within the restrictions of our own abilities and environment, we are all searching for power, and the methods we employ to seize it are not always pretty to watch.

Adler's theory presents the rough side of the human personality. Unlike the gentler images of Rogers and White who would have us reaching upward for fulfillment, Adler perceives the human race as being chased from behind by the dark specter of inferiority.

Like it or not, it is a part of ourselves that has to be faced. Neither Adler's search for power nor the need for achievement, which we will discuss shortly, presents the competitive forces which drive us on in their most attractive and benevolent light. But the competition that exists between human beings—especially in the field of something so specifically competition-orientated as sport—forms an intrinsic and absolutely indispensable part of our quest for success.

When you face a true competitor on a tennis court, you can feel his force of will and know he is out to beat you, no matter what you do or how long it takes. It is somewhat frightening. I know because I've been there, both as the instigator and the recipient of that competitive drive.

Along with Connors, Pancho Gonzalez was a prime example of the ultimately efficient tennis competitor. He had the personality of a timber wolf when he was the world's best player. As a social being, he was sometimes extremely unpleasant, although he has mellowed tremendously in recent years.

In those days, he continually browbeat the other players and tried to dominate everybody all the time. He was forever issuing challenges and was happy only when his foot was on somebody's neck. He would become as violently angry when he lost at cards as he did when he lost at tennis, railing at the blind luck of the victor and giving no one credit for anything.

Gonzalez, who shares with Connors the complex makeup of an insecure, mistrustful, driven man, is an exceptional example because, like Connors today, he sat on top of an exceptional heap of athletes.

All top tennis players, be they ranked 1, 10, or 100, have similar competitive tendencies, although most of them cloak these instincts in ways that are more socially acceptable. While they may appear charming, easygoing and even docile if you met them at a cocktail party, their affable facades would conceal a lust for conflict lurking just below the surface. Give them a chance to compete at anything anytime and they seize it. If you resist them verbally or physically, their instinct is to press forward.

Any outlet for this compulsive urge will do. They compete among each other at cards, at backgammon, at knocking down bottles in an amusement park or at trying to get a date with a pretty girl. They argue about everything. They have the instincts of game cocks.

Ninety percent of it is done in a spirit of good-natured banter but, knowing each other as they do, no one bothers to hide the fact that he feels just a tiny bit happier when he wins one of those otherwise meaningless games or arguments.

And when the time comes for the real competition on court, friendship is temporarily suspended. The fierceness of the battle, sometimes verging on antagonism, is genuine.

Gonzalez and Connors, again the extreme examples, are incapable of regarding their opponents as anything less than enemies. Although Connors is a

34

scrupulously fair fighter on court, he is, nonetheless, antagonistic toward his opponent. Once, when he was playing 36-year-old Bob Hewitt in the Alan King Classic at Caesars Palace, the fact that he could win that particular match any way he wanted did not interest him. He didn't want to just beat Hewitt, he wanted to demolish him. Boasted Jimmy to a group of us seated courtside, "I've run him 10 miles this set and I'll run him 20 the next."

The need for achievement is the desire to reach a standard of excellence in order to gain reward.

This is the champion's competitive streak showing its most unattractive face, yet, as a player myself, I cannot pretend not to recognize it. During the course of a match, I often hated my opponent. He might have been my best friend—and sometimes was. But it made no difference. Even if he made a great shot, I gave him no credit in my mind. I felt as though he were trying to take the bread out of my mouth.

Are these relentless, antagonistic and competitive urges indicative of an underlying insecurity, as Adler says? To answer this question, I have given extensive personality tests to 26 of the world's top tournament players. The results are discussed in some detail in the next chapter; but in summary, yes, the players do appear to have an underlying insecurity, as well as aggressive and competitive instincts which are higher than normal.

The need for achievement. The need for achievement is the final factor to be considered with respect to overall drive level. It is not, however, synonymous with the antagonistic urges just described. It is, by definition, "the desire to reach a standard of excellence *in order to gain reward.*"

In many ways, it is similar to Harry S. Sullivan's concept that we want to achieve goals to make other people think well of us. This, in turn, makes us think well of ourselves and, in essence, it improves our self-images.

Unlike White's striving for competence or Rogers' drive for self-actualization, the need for achievement

With high-achieving boys, the mothers took a forceful role pushing, encouraging, rewarding and punishing.

is not an instinctive part of our makeup. It is learned in early childhood.

Various types of tests have been designed to measure this need for achievement and studies have shown that children who receive high scores are likely to make successful competitors in all walks of life. They are the "pushers." They do well in school, sports and business. They are the type of people who carry their whole society upward with them in their quest for success.

Studies involving the need for achievement have produced some of the most impressive and interesting work in recent psychological literature. Some of these tests have shown that high achievers are produced by parents who expect their children to show an early independence and who set difficult standards for them. They reward their children for doing well with affection and are unhappy with failure.

With boys, in particular, it has been shown that there is a drastic difference depending on which parent does the pushing. In an oft-quoted study by B. Rosen and R. D'Andrade done in 1959, boys tested for achievement drive were divided into two groups— high and low achievers. They were brought into the laboratory and told to compete in a variety of tasks. Both parents were asked to be present and to participate. With the high-achieving boys, Rosen and D'Andrade noticed that the mothers took a forceful role "pushing, encouraging, rewarding and punishing." The fathers, meanwhile, seemed content to let the boys work on their own.

With the low-achieving boys the pattern was reversed—the fathers dominated and pushed, while the mothers stood back. Apparently, the concerned mother is able to impress her own standards on her son—interestingly, often rewarding him with physical affection. On the other hand, the domineering father seems to pose a threat and, in fact, holds his son down.

Noting that a high incidence of seafaring nations

have shown rapid increases in economic growth at various stages of their history, the American psychologist, David McClelland, has hypothesized that when the fathers go to sea in ships, the achievement need of subsequent generations seems to increase. The ancient Greeks, early Etruscans, British, Japanese and Scandinavians provide telling examples.

Mothers have traditionally played a far more prominent—and successful—role on the tennis circuit than fathers.

McClelland follows through with the theory that, as many of these ancient civilizations began to luxuriate in the fruits of their endeavors, the dominant fathers returned home; the children were placed in the care of slaves and servants to be coddled and indulged, and the need for achievement markedly declined.

Coincident with this decline, which was measured by analysis of children's books and literature of the times, the economies and political influence of these nations also fell dramatically.

It would be glib and misleading to suggest that, as tennis champions have a high need for achievement, all of them have dominant mothers and retiring fathers. There will certainly be exceptions because, as with most psychological theories, the phenomena are so complex. However, mothers have traditionally played a far more prominent—and successful—role on the tennis circuit than fathers. There have been some obvious and somewhat extreme examples over the years.

Most obvious of all, perhaps, has been the relationship between Connors and his mother, Gloria, which takes the whole thesis to its extremity. I particularly remember a scene at the Beverly Hills Tennis Club one day shortly after Connors had broken up with Marjorie Wallace. Mrs. Connors was sitting on the arm of a chair behind her son, soothingly massaging his neck and saying, "Don't worry about it, Jimbo, girls are like streetcars. There's another one coming along every five minutes." To anyone who has observed them, there has never been any doubt of the extent to which Jimmy Connors has been rewarded physically, emotionally and psychologically by his adoring mother.

My own case was a good example. My father died when I was 10 and I was the apple of my mother's eye. She constantly pushed me to achieve but was very kind and affectionate.

She would say, "What have you done today to better yourself?" It seemed as though there was always something more that could be done and she was lavish in her praise when I did it. She was the typical "Jewish Mother." It seems to be quite possible that this remarkable species of womanhood called the Jewish Mother has been largely responsible for the unusual degree of productivity and achievement of the Jewish people.

Eddie Dibbs, a gutsy, driven competitor who was ranked as No. 5 in the world during 1978, has been heavily influenced throughout his life by his mother (Dibbs, however, is of Lebanese extraction and not Jewish as is often thought), while one of the most notorious mother-son relationships involved the former No. 1 British star, Bobby Wilson. In the 50's, no British Davis Cup captain in his right mind would allow the brilliant and highly strung Wilson to take the court without his mother in attendance. It was a well-proven fact that Bobby played better when Mrs. Wilson was there.

To give further strength to this argument, there have been two sad cases in recent years in which highly talented teenagers, one from Britain and one from Australia, found themselves quite unable to generate the drive and discipline required to make the most of their abilities. One has slumped back into the lower echelons of the satellite circuits after some promising wins, while the other does not even play the circuit any more. Both had demanding, overbearing fathers.

There is a message here for parents. Although the evidence is not conclusive, nor will it hold with each individual case, it is reasonable to assume that a lov-

38

ing, supportive mother who pushes her son to early independence can help produce a child with a high need for achievement. At the same time, a domineering father can create problems. Fathers should encourage, applaud, support and generally take an interest, but they should be careful not to dominate and demand.

> **Fathers should encourage, applaud, support and generally take an interest, but they should be careful not to dominate and demand.**

A mother presents no threat to her son, because he is not trying to emulate her. That is not the case with the father. Unless the relationship is handled with love and care and restraint, the father will present too giant a figure for the son to handle. Instead of growing in his father's shadow, he will shrink.

It is more difficult to make general statements about how the need for achievement develops in women, although we know it is quite different from men. Unfortunately, virtually all the research has been done on males. Since achievement need is learned, culturally determined sex roles are very important. Although it is changing to some extent, our culture has decreed that men be aggressive, competitive and successful, while women be supportive, submissive and socially acceptable. For this reason, achievement need measured in women has been found to gradually decrease in the years after they finish school and marry. We do know that parents who urge and expect their daughters to do well and be productive create achievers. But there is no theoretical reason to believe that you can simply reverse roles and claim that a dominant father will encourage need for achievement in a daughter whereas a dominant mother will suppress it.

It is true, however, that role reversal occurs to a certain extent in that daughters are often drawn toward their fathers and see their mothers as rivals. This is called the Electra complex and contrasts with the Oedipus complex in which boys are drawn toward their mothers and view their fathers as rivals.

Even if you emerged from childhood without a high need for achievement, it may not be too late to develop it—provided that you feel such a drive is desirable. It does, after all, tend to lead to ulcers and high blood pressure.

Acquiring a high need for achievement as an adult is possible, although scientific research on the subject is far from complete. Basically, it requires a change in your thinking process; a reorganization of your priorities. You need to break down habitual thought patterns, placing greater importance on goals, so that certain aspects of life's continuing puzzle take on different values.

Tests were carried out on college students and businessmen in which they were given specific achievement training. As a result, school grades improved and the businessmen began working longer hours and were more aggressive in getting new business, increasing their authority and moving upward within their firms. How did they do it? Simply by getting together in groups for various periods of time to talk and think specifically about achievement. They were encouraged to discuss their fantasies about it, to set specific goals for themselves, to act out roles and play games involving achievement. By doing this, they became accustomed to focusing on achievement and simply rearranging their priorities, with achievement taking the highest position.

So although the need for achievement is best learned early in life, it is still possible to increase it later on. The main point to remember is the need to turn the thought processes in the direction of goal-orientated subjects and to discuss those subjects in concentrated fashion whenever possible. Parents should do this with children, a husband with his wife. A group of close friends can set up discussion sessions to talk about specific goals.

In an informal way, the tournament players on the pro circuit do this very thing. They sit around at the courts and talk endlessly about tennis—old matches, recent matches, strategy, analysis of each other's weaknesses and strengths. You name it and, providing it has to do with winning tennis matches, they talk about it. It drives their wives crazy, but it

40

does serve to involve themselves ever deeper into the game, keeping their drive level high.

If you are by nature shy and have difficulty opening up to people, start out by setting yourself personal, private goals each day and then, to put yourself on the line, include other people in them. Promise ahead of time to do something for a friend, thereby locking yourself into a commitment. Then be sure you do it. Slowly you will find habits and priorities changing. You will start thinking differently.

This new thought process will eventually spill over into your sporting activities. Your drive will be greater, your need for achievement higher. Winning on a tennis court will become a real goal instead of something you fear. You will begin competing to the limit of your potential. You might even just get an inkling of what it feels like to be Jimmy Connors.

THE BASIC ELEMENTS OF WINNING
To summarize, the component parts required for winning are:

Confidence: Get your share of victories. Seek out players you can beat as well as those who are better than you. Avoid accepting regular invitations to play with someone who is going to blow you off the court. Don't let yourself become fodder for somebody else's confidence drive.

Fulfillment: This covers the same area as self-actualization. The role of the parents is crucial here. They should not suppress the child's natural instincts but should offer strong encouragement once self-motivated activity choices have been made.

The need for achievement: This is learned and involves a reorganization of the thinking processes if it is to be substantially developed in later years. Basically, this involves a change in priorities so that goals and advancement are highlighted.

Both fulfillment, or self-actualization, and the need for achievement come under the heading of Drive but it is important to understand the basic differences between them. As an example, take two different types of mornings in your life, the kind most of us have experienced at one time or another, as we set out for a run.

First, picture a clear blue sky, crisp air and soft grass. You run easily and smoothly, gliding from step to step, breathing deeply and feeling your body functioning to perfection. That is self-actualization—running for its own sake just because it feels good. No need for set goals, times or distances. They would spoil the spirit of the morning and dampen the joy of your mood.

And now the other type of morning, when a dank, dark dawn struggles to impose day over night and you have your set three miles to run through cold, deserted streets before an early breakfast. Bed is still beckoning as you push yourself out into the damp air. Breathing quickly becomes labored and your body aches. Each step is an effort. But you drive yourself on and eventually complete your own little torture track within the time you set yourself.

Back in the kitchen, nursing a cup of coffee, you suddenly feel great. Why? Because you have satisfied your need for achievement. You have attained a goal which you feel to be valuable.

You get social approval (or at least imagined social approval) by managing to mention your run in casual conversation around the office later in the day.

"What, you went for a run on a filthy morning like this?" someone will say, just as you hoped they would. And inwardly you will glow with pride. It was hell while it lasted but, whatever else happened during the day, the memory of that otherwise insignificant achievement will remain with you.

This need for achievement is in all of us and it is no use pretending it does not exist. So set a goal, no matter what type it is or how banal it may seem. It is merely a way of activating the drives that we all possess and by doing so you can build your confidence and set yourself off on the path to becoming a winner.

CHAPTER 3.
PERSONALITIES
OF CHAMPIONS

Throughout this book various personality characteristics of tennis professionals are discussed. They are used as examples because, it is assumed, the characteristics they display are those of "winners." For the most part, this is based on scattered personal observations. It is certainly possible that on closer, more rigorous examination there may be no real, systematic psychological differences between the tennis pros and everybody else. Success on the courts might result simply because they have superior physical ability—coordination, balance, eyesight, etc. But I had personally seen too many gifted athletes beaten consistently by lesser physical specimens to believe this was true. Harold Solomon, Brian Gottfried, Dick Stockton and Roscoe Tanner are good athletes, but certainly not great ones. Probably half the college tennis teams in this country have a player or two who is their physical equal or superior. Why then have certain players been so successful?

WHAT MAKES A TRUE CHAMPION DIFFERENT?
To try to answer this, I administered a personality inventory test, the 16 P.F. Test, to 26 of the world's top players. Among these were Gonzalez, Stockton, Tan-

ner, Bob Lutz, and Stan Smith. The full list is produced on page 51.

The 16 P.F. Test has been widely used for many years. Devised by the renowned analytical psychologist, Raymond Cattell, it was first published in 1949. Since then it has been refined and validated across cultures, ages and a tremendous variety of segments of the population. The advantage of using this test is that I was able to compare the scores of the tennis pros with the normal scores of other people of the same age and sex. The differences were what interested me most.

With his test, Dr. Cattell attempted to define and measure all the important aspects of the human personality, a task that might, at first glance, appear too complicated to be possible. But as Drs. S. Karson and J. O'Dell say in their book, *The Clinical Use of the 16 P.F.*, "The really clever thing about the construction of the 16 P.F., and, it might be added, many of the other tests in Cattell's armamentarium, was that he was able to see the forest for the trees. For it should be obvious that there really is not an infinite number of ways in which people can be described. There are only the ways for which the English language provides words, specifically adjectives, and one can obtain a complete listing of all these words at the local bookstore in what is called a dictionary."

Among the approximately 4,000 adjectives are all the words used by all the literary masters to describe their characteristics—self-seeking, capricious, humorous, volatile, etc. By using complex mathematical analysis to remove synonyms and redundancies, Cattell ultimately arrived at 16 categories which define the most important aspects of the human personality.

Recent work in the field of psychological testing has cast some doubt on Cattell's assumption that the human personality can be broken down into a limited number of measurable "traits." On the other hand, in reviewing the test results of the players that I have known on a close personal basis myself, I found that

44

the tests gave pictures of almost uncanny accuracy. Therefore, I am basically convinced that these tests show that there are real personality differences between top tennis professionals and average people.

The 16 P.F. Test that I used included 187 questions with multiple-choice answers. Some examples are:

I can find enough energy to face my difficulties:
  a) always   b) generally   c) seldom
Money can buy almost everything:
  a) yes   b) uncertain   c) no
If I am called in by my boss, I:
  a) make it a chance to ask for something I want
  b) in between
  c) fear I've done something wrong
In social contacts I:
  a) show my emotions as I wish
  b) in between
  c) keep my emotions to myself
I get tense as I think of all the things lying ahead of me:
  a) yes   b) sometimes   c) no
The pomp and splendor of any big state ceremony are things which should be preserved:
  a) yes   b) in between   c) no
I am always a sound sleeper, never walking or talking in my sleep:
  a) yes   b) in between   c) no

When the answers are analyzed each individual receives a score on each of 16 personality characteristics. I took the average for all players and have plotted them on the chart on pages 46–47.

Are you supercharged like the pros? Analyzing the chart reveals that the most outstanding characteristic of these top players is their high level of anxiety and drive. This is indicated by their high scores on Q4, which averaged higher than any other score on the test. Quoting Karson and O'Dell, "The high Q4 person admits to tension, difficulty in calming down, inability to tolerate criticism, sleeplessness, concern

Scales showing the average scores of 26 professional tennis players on the 16 P.F. Test

FACTOR	LOW SCORE DESCRIPTION	AVERAGE			SIGNIF. ABOVE AVERAGE		HIGH SCORE DESCRIPTION
		5.0	5.5	6.0	6.5	7.0	
A	RESERVED, DETACHED, CRITICAL, ALOOF, STIFF (Sizothymia)	X					OUTGOING, WARM-HEARTED, EASYGOING, PARTICIPATING (Affectothymia)
B	LESS INTELLIGENT, CON-CRETE-THINKING (Lower scholastic mental capacity)				X		MORE INTELLIGENT, AB-STRACT-THINKING, BRIGHT (Higher scholastic mental capacity)
C	EMOTIONALLY STABLE, MATURE, FACES REALITY, CALM (Higher ego strength)			X			AFFECTED BY FEELINGS, EMOTIONALLY LESS STABLE, EASILY UPSET CHANGEABLE (Lower ego strength)
E	HUMBLE, MILD, EASILY LED, DOCILE, ACCOMMODATING (Submissiveness)				X		ASSERTIVE, AGGRESSIVE, STUBBORN, COMPETITIVE (Dominance)
F	SOBER, TACITURN, SERIOUS (Desurgency)		X				HAPPY-GO-LUCKY, ENTHUSIASTIC (Surgency)
G	EXPEDIENT, DISREGARDS RULES (Weaker superego strength)	X					CONSCIENTIOUS, PER-SISTENT, MORALISTIC, STAID (Stronger superego strength)
H	SHY, TIMID, THREAT-SENSITIVE (Threctia)		X				VENTURESOME, UNIN-HIBITED, SOCIALLY BOLD (Parmia)
I	TOUGH-MINDED, SELF-RELIANT, REALISTIC (Harria)			X			TENDER-MINDED, SEN-SITIVE, CLINGING, OVERPROTECTED (Premsia)

Adapted from 16 P.F. test profile, copyright © 1956 and 1973 by the Institute For Personality And Ability Testing.

FACTOR	LOW SCORE DESCRIPTION	AVERAGE			SIGNIF. ABOVE AVERAGE		HIGH SCORE DESCRIPTION
		5.0	5.5	6.0	6.5	7.0	
L	TRUSTING, ACCEPTING CONDITIONS (Alaxia)				X		SUSPICIOUS, HARD TO FOOL (Protension)
M	PRACTICAL, "DOWN-TO-EARTH" CONCERNS (Praxemia)	X					IMAGINATIVE, BOHE-MIAN, ABSENT-MINDED (Autia)
N	FORTHRIGHT, UNPRE-TENTIOUS, GENUINE BUT SOCIALLY CLUMSY (Artlessness)	X					ASTUTE, POLISHED, SOCIALLY AWARE (Shrewdness)
O	SELF-ASSURED, PLACID, SECURE, COMPLACENT, SERENE (Untroubled adequacy)		X				APPREHENSIVE, SELF-REPROACHING, INSE-CURE, WORRYING, TROUBLED (Guilt proneness)
Q^1	CONSERVATIVE, RE-SPECTING TRADITIONAL IDEAS (Conservatism of temperament)			X			EXPERIMENTING, LIB-ERAL, FREE-THINKING (Radicalism)
Q^2	GROUP-DEPENDENT, A "JOINER" AND SOUND FOLLOWER (Group adherence)				X		SELF-SUFFICIENT, RE-SOURCEFUL, PREFERS OWN DECISIONS (Self-sufficiency)
Q^3	CONTROLLED, EXACTING WILL POWER, SOCIALLY PRECISE, COMPULSIVE (High Strength of self-sentiment)				X		UNDISCIPLINED SELF-CONFLICT, LAX, FOL-LOWS URGES, CARELESS OF SOCIAL RULES (Low integration)
Q^4	RELAXED, TRANQUIL, UNFRUSTRATED, COM-POSED (Low ergic tension)					X	TENSE, FRUSTRATED, DRIVEN, OVERWROUGHT (High ergic tension)

All scores were first converted to STEN scores and averaged. Statistical significance was determined at the .05 level.

about future happenings, an admission of not holding one's tongue at the proper times and similar items. Q4 may well be the most important single indicator of acute neurotic trends on the 16 P.F." Many of the items have clear "good" or "bad" answers and are, therefore, easily faked. In essence, to get a high Q4 one has to openly admit being very anxious. Karson and O'Dell in their clinical work say that one should "always take a high Q4 score seriously."

This anxiety does not reach the levels nor appear in the dissociated form which would lead to clinical symptoms. In fact, in this case, it appears to be directed and acts as a motivator. It drives the players on past the point of normal endurance. It keeps them on the practice courts working on weaknesses—unwilling to accept mediocrity. It forces them past the pain barrier.

Several other scores are also indicative of anxiety, and the players scored significantly in the direction of anxiety on nearly all of them. These were C, L and Q3. Of these, L is the most interesting and goes beyond mere anxiety. Quoting again from Karson and O'Dell, "Factor L is the most indicative of disturbance of all the P.F. scales. Someone obtaining a high score on L insists on getting his point across, feels that people are talking about him behind his back, cannot endure human frailties, is oppositional, likely to fight, antagonistic and quick to take offense, to paraphrase some of the items. This is clearly the common psychiatric syndrome of paranoia, if carried to the extreme."

In fact, the players certainly do not usually carry it to the extreme, although my personal observations have verified many of the above characteristics. The players do quickly and vigorously jump to the fray if they perceive someone as an antagonist. They are not at all the types to be pushed around easily. However, it rarely comes to this. Since they are well-known athletes, people generally treat them well and they don't encounter much to be antagonistic about. Off the tennis court, they see each other as comrades in arms, movie and dinner mates and sharers of experiences. Despite what one might think from their test scores, the locker room is generally a place of good fellowship. But on the court, all that ends. They are antagonists and there are no two ways about it. Then, all the submerged fighting energy surfaces and focuses on winning.

> On the court, all the submerged fighting energy surfaces and focuses on winning.

Connors is a fine example of someone with this type of personality trait, carried to a greater extreme than with most players. He has always been, although to a lesser extent recently, a loner. For years, his natural tendency toward suspicion and paranoia bound him to his mother and one-time agent, Bill Riordan, and isolated him from the rest of the players. In 1974, the year Connors won Wimbledon, Forest Hills and the Australian championships, his battles ranged well beyond the tennis court. In fact, it was only after a great deal of negotiating and legal expense that they were kept out of the law courts. Within that 12-month period, he was involved in suits against Arthur Ashe, Jack Kramer, Donald Dell, the French Tennis Federation and, in fact, the tennis players' own association, the ATP.

With people that Connors considers to be friends, he is a perfectly likeable guy. The trouble is that there aren't many of them. One of his criteria for friendship is that the friend must not be perceived as trying to take advantage of him or benefit materially from the relationship.

As for evidence of anxiety, most of the top players display it openly in their mannerisms. John McEnroe, Tom Okker, Eddie Dibbs, Jimmy Connors and Ilie Nastase, to name a few, are hyper, restless personalities who have difficulty sitting still, who talk in short bursts and who are generally just "twitchy." Even Arthur Ashe who, to the outside world, appears to be "Mr. Cool," often conceals a stomach churning and knotted with tension. I feel free to name names here, because none of the players mentioned above took the test. However, personal association has shown me

49

The tendency toward criticism will keep the pros working on a weakness in their games long after other players would have quit.

that they fit the pattern. They would probably have scored higher than the players we did test.

Exercising independence. Among the other traits on which the players scored highly are those which indicate independence and dislike of authority. These are shown by the combination of high scores on L (Suspiciousness), Q2 (Self-sufficiency), and E (Dominance). What better trait for an individual, lonely sport. If you are not able to hold yourself together well enough to win, no one else can do it for you.

Of course, the high score on E (Dominance) requires some comment. An individual with this trait is characterized by Karson and O'Dell as a person who, "enjoys dominating and controlling others, as well as criticizing them. Such a person likes being in command, enjoys meeting challenges, feels superior to others, and does not mind forcing his ideas on other people. Indeed he enjoys it!" The tendency toward criticism shows up as a type of perfectionism, and applies to their own imperfections as well. It will keep them working on a weakness in their games long after other types would have quit. As for the usefulness of the urge to dominate and control another person, in tennis this hardly needs elaboration.

Hardly dumb athletes. The players also are significantly more intelligent than the average person. Out of the 26 players we tested, all but one were average or above. However, this may relate less to the game itself than it does to the fact that tennis is still a sport that draws its participants mainly from the middle and upper classes.

If the professional players' psychological profiles were interesting, the half dozen players' wives we tested were even more so! (See list, next page.) In addition to being good-looking, they displayed a whole range of attractive psychological qualities. They were all far above average in intelligence, and most were highly venturesome, emotionally stable, enthu-

50

siastic and free-thinking. It is not difficult to understand how men as sought-after as the pro tennis players fell in love with such women.

PLAYERS TESTED

1. John Austin
2. Michael Fishbach
3. Peter Fleming
4. Richard (Pancho) Gonzalez
5. Thomas Gullikson
6. Timothy Gullikson
7. Chico Hagey
8. Johan Kriek
9. John Lloyd
10. Robert C. Lutz
11. Bruce Manson
12. Ray Moore
13. Jan E. Norback
14. Douglas Palm
15. Willem Prinsloo
16. Dennis Ralston
17. Martin Riessen
18. David Schneider
19. Stan Smith
20. Sherwood Stewart
21. Richard Stockton
22. Roscoe Tanner
23. Brian Teacher
24. Eliot Teltscher
25. Trey Waltke
26. Kim Warwick

WIVES TESTED

1. Carole Dell
2. Rosemary Gullikson (Tim)
3. April Riessen
4. Linda Ann Stewart
5. Lailee van Dillen

CHAPTER 4.
GETTING
READY TO WIN

GETTING THE WINNING EDGE
WITH A PLANNED ROUTINE

The green curtain at the back of the court parted and semifinalists Tom Okker and Ray Moore emerged side by side, walking briskly. Some observant spectators might have noticed that they were walking *very* briskly.

By the time the two players were halfway to the umpire's chair at the Paris Indoor Championships, "brisk" no longer described the unusual pace at which Okker and Moore were proceeding. The expressions on their faces were becoming more strained with each lengthening stride. Could this be a race?

"You bet it was a race," said Moore. "It was a race to see who could reach his 'lucky' chair first, although, of course, neither of us wanted to admit it. I had played well in that tournament, beating Vilas and Tanner, and on both those occasions I had sat to the left of the umpire. Apparently, Tom had been using that side during his matches as well. Neither of us wanted to risk breaking the routine, so here we were engaged in this farce of trying to reach a certain spot on the court before the other guy when we were supposed to be walking calmly side by side. At the last moment, that bloody Okker broke all the rules and sprinted the last couple of yards, so of course I had no chance. I mean the man's as quick as a hare. I was livid!"

How superstitions are helpful. Tennis is rife with superstitions as are many pro sports. Much of the superstitious behavior players engage in on a tennis court appears to be useless, but it is not. Although superstition is, in psychological terms, the misapplication of cause and effect, it can be beneficial. Often, it supplies structure in preparing for a match and therefore has its value.

The popular Indian champion, Vijay Amritraj, whose lifestyle is molded by a whole range of superstitious beliefs, derives structure from a highly intricate system which pays heed to neither logic nor reason. He believes that if he wins his first match, he must repeat his pre-match routine in exact detail to perpetuate his luck in the matches that follow. Sometimes it necessitates locking himself into an incredibly strict and often highly inconvenient pre-match routine.

This was the case when Amritraj won both the singles and doubles titles in Mexico City in the fall of 1978. He had risen early the first morning because of a two-hour time change and was doomed to get up every morning thereafter at 7:00, even though he was playing evening matches. Breakfast had to be taken at 9:30 and it had to consist of orange juice, two eggs over-medium, sausage and white toast.

Between 7:00 and 8:30 in the evening he had to watch television whether or not there was anything interesting, because that was what he had done on the first day. Depending on his playing schedule, dinner every night was at 9:00 and every night it was Enchiladas Rojas.

But worst of all, in defiance of all his professional instincts and training, Amritraj did not practice all week. There had been no time to have a hit on that opening day so that was it. No practice.

"Sounds ridiculous, doesn't it?" he laughs. "But that's the way I am. It's more important for me psychologically to follow a routine based on superstition than to do the obvious things I know I should be doing—like having a hit before my matches."

That superstitious streak runs so deep in Amritraj that, even when he tried to break his self-imposed rules and practice before meeting Raul Ramirez in the final, he immediately felt guilty and couldn't keep a ball in court.

"After three or four minutes of spraying balls all over the place, I packed it in," said Amritraj. "And when Raul won the first game at love I started to worry about it. I just knew I shouldn't have practiced, although technically I needed to."

Once he put that worry out of his mind, Amritraj achieved the considerable feat of beating Ramirez in front of his home crowd not only in singles but in doubles, too, later in the day with brother Anand.

For anyone unfettered by the rigorous demands of Eastern mystique, a routine such as Vijay set for himself in Mexico City would be ruinous. But that is not the point. In matters of superstition it is each to his own. Psychologically, Amritraj was better tuned for his matches by doing all the crazy things he did, just as Okker was happier sitting in his "lucky" chair in Paris.

Stupid? Not at all. For both players it was part of a routine that calmed the mind and as such was beneficial. In fact, as far as pre-match preparation is concerned, *any* routine is beneficial. It is psychologically better to have a routine in which you do things that are useless than to have no routine at all.

Doctors have discovered that it is possible to cure patients of a whole range of ailments—some as serious as paralysis or deafness—though prescribing a totally useless drug which works *only* because the sufferer believes it will. This phenomenon, called the "placebo effect," is purely psychological, but the results are definitely real.

Of course, the placebo effect doesn't always work

54

in medicine or in tennis. Vitas Gerulaitis doesn't always win the next game when he carefully avoids walking in the doubles alley while changing ends. And the South African, John Yuill, doesn't produce an ace every time he serves, although one might think he had a neurological deformity, because the stutter-step in his walk as he goes back to serve is so pronounced and consistent. In fact, Yuill is simply breaking stride to avoid touching the baseline with his foot. It serves no purpose other than to make him *think* he will serve better. As all practitioners of the art are quite ready to admit, logic plays no part in superstition.

Of course, they are far better off if the ingredients of any superstitious routine are effective physically as well as psychologically. The benefits will, inevitably, be restricted if it is made up simply of putting the left sock on before the right or bowing three times to the East.

Believe in your routine. Being in good physical condition, eating the right things at the right time, and having a clear mind and match plan offer a far more solid foundation to the structure that should surround match preparation. And no matter who you are or where you are going to play, the importance of that structure does not vary. Be it in a competitive match on the local public park courts or in the final of the U.S. Open, the player who has devised a structured preparation is going to start with an edge.

Former Wimbledon champion Tony Trabert spelled this out for me when we talked about pre-match nerves during the 1978 Arco Open in Los Angeles. He told me that he did not have many problems with nerves during his days of competition. Occasionally, he would be slightly nervous at the beginning of a match, but this would soon go away and rarely return. I asked him how he managed to be so tranquil.

"Because I was always so well prepared," he replied. "I always went on court knowing that I'd done everything in my power to prepare myself to play. I

55

was in better physical condition and had worked on my strokes more systematically than my opponents."

Who knows whether Trabert was in better shape than his opponents or had prepared more carefully? The important thing was that *he* believed it and from this belief he derived both physical and mental strength.

Everybody needs something to grasp onto in order to give him strength under conditions of uncertainty. Some philosophers have said that this is the basis of religion. We are generally aware of our own pervasive inadequacies. We need some indefinable power to tell us what to do and to calm our fears. Some benevolent power that is infinitely knowledgeable where we are ignorant, that is infinitely strong where we are weak, to give us shelter and support. During the dawn of history, when the first religions took root, man was dominated by ruthless natural forces. People were ignorant and the fear that sprung from that ignorance demanded relief. Calamities occurred that went way beyond man's understanding and, in his panic, he ran for shelter. As has been said so often, if God had not existed, man would have invented him.

The shelter offered by religion is constructed of belief. The benefits it offers are spiritual and psychological. Yet, time and again they have proved themselves stronger than brick and mortar.

A tennis court offers no shelter. There is no wall to back up against, no ropes to lean on, no corner to crouch in. You are fighting out in the open, totally exposed. There is no one to turn to for help, so you must rely on your own strength. When you walk out on that court, you need strong psychological armor and your belief in that armor will definitely have a powerful influence over the way you play. Basically, you need to *feel* you have an "edge."

A recommended pre-match routine. At Pepperdine University where I coach the tennis team, I try to give my players a security or edge that is structured on
56

a complete routine which incorporates a set pattern consisting of:

1. *Timing*—when to arrive at the courts.
2. *Eating*—what and when to eat.
3. *Physical*—stretching and warm-up.
4. *Dress*—what to wear.
5. *Plan*—match strategy.

Although the average non-competition player does not have the flexibility of members of a college team, it is worthwhile to examine the routine the team follows because it is a good framework from which to understand the preparation process.

HOME Matches: Players have lunch two hours before match time.

The team gathers dressed and ready to play one hour before match time. For fifteen minutes they do their routine sequence of stretching exercises. Then they hit and warm up all strokes for half an hour. Finally, we retire to our "ready room" in the gymnasium, where it is warm, quiet and isolated. There the strategy for the six individual singles matches is discussed. To increase motivation, we talk about the importance of the match in our season's plans.

Five minutes before match time we are at the courts.

AWAY Matches: We arrive at least an hour before lunch or approximately three hours before match time. Immediately on arrival we have a 45-minute warm-up to get used to the courts.

We have lunch, relax and return to the courts 45 minutes before match time. We then follow the same sequence as we do at home, except that the hit is 15 minutes instead of a half hour and, since we have no ready room, we must find some secluded place to have our strategy session.

In this way the team goes into the match physically warm and mentally focused on the task at hand.

Many teams make the mistake of arriving at an away match literally five minutes before match time. When they walk out on court, their heads are still in the car somewhere, back down the road. By the time their minds arrive, their bodies are often a set behind. As home coach that suits me fine.

Timing: Notice that in the sequence we follow, the players' minds are brought deeper and deeper into the tennis step by step. Their thinking processes cannot be detached from their school books and personal problems at the spin of a racquet. The very deepening process has to be achieved methodically, stage by stage.

There is psychological back-up for this phenomenon. Johann Herbart in the early 1800's advanced the theory that the sum of the ideas already present in the conscious mind controls the entry of new ideas into consciousness.

Herbart maintained that new ideas were drawn passively into consciousness if they were similar to the ideas already existing. If they were inconsistent, they were rejected. The more ideas of a particular type there are, the more likely it is that additional ideas of the same type will be drawn in. The concept is much like a magnetic core attracting magnetic particles. As each new particle is added, the size and the overall attractive power of the core is increased, thereby helping it draw in additional particles of similar subject matter.

The need to change the mass of thoughts of my Pepperdine players from school to tennis is the underlying reason for the length of our team's preparation. The change takes time.

Richard Mosk, a friend of mine who is a member of the Beverly Hills Tennis Club, tells me that the inability to put business worries out of their minds during matches is the most common complaint among members at the club. They cannot single-mindedly focus on the match they are playing, because errant thoughts of business keep forcing their way in. Just as my players' brains may be loaded with the intricacies of calculus and economics as they come out of their classrooms, so a businessman's mind may be filled with details of a client's contract or an insurance problem—a mass of complex thoughts that have collected and solidified into a hard core through hours of concentrated work. None of these thoughts will be changed quickly under conditions of disorder and stress. And disorder is what a player gets when he shows up for the match with five minutes to spare and comes rushing out of the locker room with unlaced shoes, zipping up his pants.

It is of primary importance to arrive at the courts early. A half hour before match time would be a good minimum to shoot for.

Obviously, lack of time can be a major and sometimes insurmountable problem for businessmen. But they will do better if they recognize the problem and make the greatest possible effort to overcome it within the limits imposed by their working day. They should try to schedule the most complex matters and thorniest negotiations early in the day. Then they should try to wind down their business gradually, as far in advance of the match as possible, while, at the same time, increasing their involvement in tennis by steps described in this chapter. In any case, it is of primary importance to arrive at the courts early. A half hour before match time would be a good minimum to shoot for.

Of course, this and the rest of the routine set out here is much easier to follow if you have a coach or instructor, but the club player blessed with some self-discipline can take the essence of it and use the salient features to bolster his psychological armor. But, remember, to do so, you need time.

Eating: The individual must work out by trial and error the exact timing and quantity of food to eat before a match. There are actually a few people who can put away a steak 45 minutes before they play and not have it bother them. Six hamburgers, wolfed down in quick succession, don't even seem to make a dent in Gene Mayer's appetite, which day or night, is always larger than his Prince racquet. But there is a norm for most of us and I would like to recommend that, whenever possible, a player eat one and a half to two hours before a match.

In choosing your diet, remember there are three basic types of foods:

1. Carbohydrates (CHO), which digest rapidly and supply quick energy;
2. Fats, which supply greater energy than CHO but digest more slowly, and which are good for staying power;
3. Proteins, which digest relatively slowly—faster than fat but slower than CHO; a poor source of energy, protein is used to rebuild tissues, so it is most beneficial after the match.

Your match needs are for energy—mainly for quick energy—but also for longer term energy. Therefore, your meal should consist mostly of CHO with some fats and proteins.

A couple of ham and cheese sandwiches, for example, are excellent. The bread supplies the CHO and the ham and cheese supply the fat and protein.

If you are working in the office and playing that evening, have a sandwich sent in to eat at your desk an hour or two before you are due to play. Do not load up on fats or protein. They will merely send you on court with that heavy, sluggish feeling and start you out at a disadvantage.

If you are the type who gets especially nervous before a big match, then eat a little earlier. Nerves and tension interfere with the digestive system. A whole set of biological functions are activated when the mind informs the autonomic nervous and endocrine systems of possible danger.

When this alarm system goes off, blood is forced away from the skin and digestive tract into the main arteries, causing blood pressure to increase (but decreasing the external flow of blood if you are cut). The heart rate increases. Pupils dilate. Digestion stops. The human body is then prepared for quick and powerful action.

The physical warm-up before a match serves to loosen the muscles, lower the level of nervous tension and focus your mind on your body.

The same things happen, albeit on a diluted basis, when you are nervous before a match. So take into account your slowed digestion and eat half an hour earlier—once again taking care to avoid excess fats.

If you are one of those hearty souls who likes to watch the dawn come up over your lob and therefore needs to be on court 30 minutes after leaping out of bed, a modified diet is called for. First, stay away from heavy doses of bacon and eggs. All that fat slurping around when you run for that first drop shot will make you wish you had overslept. Again, stick to carbohydrates but in smaller quantities. A couple of pieces of toast with light butter and jam, a Danish and, for extra sugar intake, some fruit juice—these are the best fuels to get the human motor ticking fast and effectively after a good night's sleep.

Physical: Pre-match exercises can take many forms, from precise stretching exercises just before you go on the court to various ways of reducing tension in the preceding hours.

The physical warm-up before a match has three purposes. One is to loosen the muscles and tendons so that movement becomes easier and the risk of injury is reduced. The second is to lower the level of nervous tension as we will discuss later on in this chapter. Third is to focus your mind on your body. This will simplify your thinking, reduce anxiety and draw your attention to the match which is about to be played.

If you are at the courts early, have a hit or, if you are feeling tense and there is no one available to hit with, go for a short jog. But be careful not to overdo it. Professional athletes, who naturally build up enormous reservoirs of stamina, may be able to hit for 45 minutes without feeling the effects, but the average amateur player may find this exhausting. So rest yourself when it doesn't matter and, if possible, try to

61

improve your stamina with some extra running.

The jogging will loosen your muscles and ease your tension. The hitting will do the same thing but, in addition, it re-accustoms your hands, eyes and body to the playing conditions.

Before the match, I recommend a concentrated series of stretching exercises. The particular positions can be obtained from various books on stretching and yoga exercises.

For my team, I use a 15-minute sequence of modified yoga stretches, which includes several positions that require body balance. We hold each position for 20 to 30 seconds. For the first 10 seconds, we simply allow the muscles to relax; for the next 10 to 20 seconds we consciously stretch the muscles.

The mental approach is extremely important during the stretch. If you fill your mind with business or various other worrisome thoughts, the muscles do not relax properly. You must make an effort to clear your mind at this time and concentrate specifically on the muscles that are being stretched. This is one reason that the balancing exercises are so useful, because the very act of having to keep your balance forces you to concentrate and focus on what you are doing.

Dress: Clothes, even tennis clothes, are a matter of personal taste. But within the accepted standards of current-day style it should be possible to recommend that you dress simply, but well, for all important matches. Dressing in a way that is both neat and normal can become part of your pre-match routine—a part of the structure that will provide you with psychological armor out there on court.

The way you dress should not add to your pressures over the match. Your clothes should meet with the approval of your fellows and thereby boost your confidence. We live in a social world and other people's values affect how we feel about ourselves. We all need approval from others, and this approval is always as we see it, because no one looks at life through the same lens. Whether they do or not, we should at least *feel* that others approve of our dress.

No matter what their nationality or social background, all the top pros take a certain pride in their appearance.

No matter what their nationality or social background, you will notice that almost all the top professionals take a certain pride in their appearance and, even though the sponsorship money many receive is no hindrance, it is often just that—pride—which is the motivating factor behind the way they look. John Newcombe is always well-groomed; Adriano Panatta and Charlie Pasarell are both stylish in their differing ways; Jaimie Fillol and Harold Solomon are invariably neat, and Ilie Nastase, who has the vast resources of Adidas at his disposal, is very particular about what he wears, always insisting on colors that coordinate properly.

Since the tennis boom began at the start of the 1970's, tenniswear has become a multimillion dollar industry. With 24 million tennis players in the United States alone, the market is huge and the competition fierce. Today's top stars are paid incredible sums of money to act as walking commercials for clothing manufacturers whose research has proven that the public at large still practices a modern form of animism. Going back to the dawn of history, animism is the belief that spiritual forces inhabit non-living objects or bodies. Primitives used this type of thinking in worshipping fire, the sun, certain animals, the moon or the stars. Some went further and ate the hearts or other organs of brave enemies to ingest the spirits of the enemies and become brave themselves.

No one genuinely believes that the spirits of Borg or Connors actually inhabit the tennis clothes that bear their names on the labels. But by buying and wearing these clothes many people, believe it or not, practice a modified type of animism—one that can often be seen in the behavior of young children.

For example, when I was a small child I was terribly impressed by the Superman movies I watched on television. I recall stealing a towel from the next-door neighbor's clothesline and using it for a cape, just like my idol, Superman. I ran around with my "cape" flapping behind me, jumping, yelling and feeling that I had superhuman powers. Maybe to the neighbors, a fat kid running around with a towel behind his neck didn't appear too superhuman. But *I* thought I looked like Superman and, reality notwithstanding, I felt very strong and good.

Since we are no longer children, our fantasies are no longer so overpowering and vivid. Nonetheless, our fantasies are not completely gone. The image we have of ourselves as looking like the tennis superstars whose clothes we wear can certainly give us a psychological boost.

Being well-turned-out should also be seen as a statement of your commitment to the match. If you are taking the match seriously, then it is logical that you prepare for it seriously. That includes taking care with your appearance; it is a show of respect to yourself and your opponent.

The image you project can also have a psychological effect on your opponent and it need not always be a comfortable one. No one was more fastidious about his appearance than the former British Davis Cup star, Mike Sangster, who was a Wimbledon and Forest Hills semifinalist in the 60's. In the middle of the most gruelling, nerve-wracking match, possibly with a wall of hysterical Italians or Spaniards hurling abuse at him in some continental cauldron in Milan or Madrid, Sangster would calmly wipe himself down during the changeover and then, with an air of infuriating British phlegm, very carefully fold his towel so that all four corners met and lay it neatly over the back of his chair. When he walked back into playing position, there was never a hair out of place or a shirttail untucked.

I don't know how many points that was worth against exhausted, highly strung opponents, but I suspect they found it very disheartening to see Sangster find so much time for seemingly irrelevant details in the middle of a do-or-die struggle.

64

But Sangster was a man who always attempted to add structure to chaos and that was one of his greatest strengths. I remember watching him play roulette in Puerto Rico, carefully charting the outcome of each spin of the wheel and stacking his chips in neat, even piles. Each wager was placed only after careful consideration of the evening's pattern at the wheel and his own betting system. I am sure he would have been terribly disturbed if he had had to deal with the fact that the numbers that come up in roulette are totally random and independent from any past events or sequences. In the realm of chance, there is nothing more chaotic or less logical than that little white ball bounding haphazardly out of those rotating slots. Yet, Sangster had managed to superimpose order on a crazy game, where none had previously existed. It made him more comfortable, gave him more confidence. It was part of the armor he carried with him through all his endeavors, and the solidity of that structure enabled him to remain rock-like—winning innumerable tight matches for Britain in the Davis Cup, for instance—while others collapsed under the mental strain.

The clothes you wear in all walks of life declare yourself. A businessman will turn up for an appointment looking smart and well-tailored because he wants to state that he is a successful and serious person. He is saying to his associates, "I am here to play our mutual game—the game of business. We will be playing by the rules we both understand and accept. We will be playing for real." People who over- or under-dress are often making a different statement. The player who arrives at the courts looking like the ultimate fashion plate may be using the occasion to display his or her fabulous clothing, rather than to play tennis. Here the dress may become a partial substitute for the tennis, a form of defensiveness. It is a way of changing the rules of the game so that the game becomes easier to win. If the rules are that to be the

Showing up for a match dressed like a bum may also be a form of defensiveness.

winner you must win two out of three sets against a determined opponent, that is tough. Your ego is substantially at risk. But if the rules are that you can win by spending $300 on clothes at the pro shop, then the only risk is that you don't have the cash or credit cards. And with credit cards arriving unsolicited in the mail these days, that's not much risk at all.

On the other hand, showing up for a match dressed like a bum may also be a form of defensiveness. It tends to be a more powerful, assertive form of defensiveness than over-dressing. It says, "I don't have to abide by your rules. I set my own." And by taking control of the rules, the down-dressers open a number of options for themselves. They can, as many upper-class Englishmen do, use it as a way of declaring their amateur status. That is why at the Queen's Club and other expensive athletic establishments in England one will see very fit-looking young men with beautiful accents turning up to play excellent games of squash or tennis in creased and shrunken shirts, dirty shorts and socks that flop around their ankles. It would not do, you see, to be taken for a professional.

They are afraid to admit that they take the game seriously. They would like to pretend it is a very casual affair in which winning or losing is of little importance. It enables them to say, "Don't expect me to be that good, old boy. I play only for fun."

On the other hand, it can be a sign of rebellion and direct antagonism toward the existing system. As a young player, this was my own attitude.

I was raised in Tucson, Ariz., and learned my tennis in a relaxed, small-town atmosphere. I knew everyone and everyone knew me. I had plenty of friends and was quite comfortable with the local tennis establishment. Then, when I was 16, I moved to southern California, the center of junior tennis in the United States and the "big time."

From the beginning, I was uncomfortable. The Southern California Tennis Association was run by

Perry T. Jones, as it had been for the preceding 50 years. He was an absolute dictator and a stickler for all kinds of rules, including "proper"dress on and off the tennis court. This meant freshly pressed all-whites for each match and coats and ties at social functions. Jones had his favorites, who were given playing privileges at the Los Angeles Tennis Club, sent to various tournaments and set up with practice matches with the pros. He was particularly fond of home-grown young men who learned their tennis under his system and who came from conservative, established upper-class families. I did not fit.

Make it easy on yourself and conform to reasonable tennis dress codes.

My first encounter with Jones was after winning the junior singles at Ojai, the second most prestigious tournament in southern California. Afterward, he called me into his office—I thought to congratulate me on my win. To my dismay, I got an hour's dressing down about the wrinkles in the shorts I wore for the finals. In the years that followed, we never got along. I insisted, as a matter of principle, on disobeying his dress requirements and he tolerated me because I won enough tournaments to bring some credit to the Southern California Tennis Association. There was always friction and, of course, I was never accorded the special "perks" which he reserved for his favorites. In hindsight, I can see that my rebellion stemmed from my own insecurities as an outsider. Although Jones was unquestionably arbitrary and dictatorial, he was not the evil man that I pictured him to be at the time. I was subconsciously convinced beforehand that I could never gain his favor, so I rejected him first and refused to play according to his rules.

In most rebellions, there is an element of defensiveness. The people who rebel often fear they cannot meet the demands of the existing system. They then set out to either change it or disregard it entirely.

As far as tennis is concerned, cut-off jeans and a brightly colored T-shirt aren't going to solve your problem. Do not add to the pressures of winning the match the pressures of fighting the established system. Make it easy on yourself and conform to reasonable tennis dress codes.

Plan: Give yourself time to think about your opponent's game before you go on court. List his or her strengths and weaknesses and consider how they can best be exploited by your own strengths.

Providing, of course, you have played this person before, think back to your previous encounter and try to picture the match. When you came to the net, were you winning more points than you were losing? Where did your opponent hit most of his passing shots, down the line or crosscourt? Who was steadier on the baseline? When he came to net, did you test his overhead?

The answers to these and other similar questions should enable you to come up with a reasonable plan of attack. If you have not played this person before, ask other people how he or she plays. Try to find out about weaknesses or strengths. Then construct a plan which will hopefully pit your strengths against your opponent's weaknesses.

Having brought all this into focus, you should then decide what you intend to do—even if you have to change it later. You must realize, of course, that the most carefully laid pre-match strategy may have to be re-evaluated during the course of the match itself. Some changes often have to be made. But to go on court without a concrete plan of action is to invite disorder and panic.

PRE-MATCH TENSION: SEEKING THE RIGHT LEVEL

Are you a high-tension or a low-tension person? In other words, do you perform better under conditions of high stress or low stress?

It's amazing how few people know themselves well enough to answer that question. Yet it's an important one for a tennis player because tension—and your individual response to it—overlies all the other elements of preparing yourself for a match.

If you're not quite sure where you stand on the tension scale, test yourself. For instance, how do you react if you are writing a long report for your boss and your secretary bursts in to tell you an important client is in town unexpectedly and will drop by in a couple of hours? Do you calmly switch gears to finish the report before the client arrives, perhaps even writing it better under the pressure of a new deadline? Or does your mind momentarily freeze in horror while you contemplate delaying the report for a day—or at the very least closing the door, turning off the phones until the few minutes before the client arrives?

> **Everyone has a characteristic level of tension which he tries to maintain, often subconsciously.**

If you work better and enjoy the extra pressure you're under, then you are a high-tension person. If not, then you fall into the low-tension category.

There are other examples. Do you work well on the run—in the backs of taxicabs and in airport lounges? Or do you prefer to allot important tasks to specific times in your day when you know you will not be disturbed? Did you cram for school exams, possibly doing your best work under the shadow of the ax? Do you schedule your day carefully so that you have extra time for travel and other contingencies? Or do you over-schedule so that things pile up, causing you to run late and become harried?

How do you perform under these conditions? Think carefully. If you tend to create tension for yourself to stimulate your performance, you are a high-stress individual. If you avoid tension whenever possible and perform poorly when it catches up with you, you are a low-stress person.

As the psychologist Salvatore Maddi noted, everyone has a characteristic level of tension which he tries to maintain, often subconsciously. If the level falls too low, he looks for stimulation. If it rises too high, he seeks tranquility. If tension is at an unaccustomed level, the individual will be uncomfortable and his performance in all probability will suffer. So whether you are a high- or low-tension individual, you must take care to be sure that your tension level reaches the proper height or depth.

What should you do if you're a high-tension type? Nastase is normally a high-tension individual. He is used to questioning linesmen, badgering opponents and playing under conditions of general furor. Before playing Borg in the 1976 Wimbledon final, Nastase had been under tremendous pressure to behave himself from the press, as well as his friends and relatives. Before the match, he vowed that he would. But to do it, he found it necessary to suppress much of his natural exuberance. By holding his emotions in check in one area, he did it in all areas, lest he lose control and allow himself to become engulfed in more arguments. Yet, when he needed to crank himself up to the proper level of tension for the big points, nothing happened. He was flat.

Afterward, he admitted that he had not even been nervous when he walked on court. Trying to behave was a laudable idea, but it proved fatal to his chances of winning the Wimbledon title. Nastase, of course, is unique in many ways; he is not, after all, your normal kind of guy. But there are plenty of players who function best under high tension as he does, and they should avoid falling into a similar trap.

So if you are a high-tension type, try not to do anything that is mentally or physically exhausting before a match, because it will have the effect of lowering tension. For instance, if you have to put in a full day's work before an important club match, try, if possible, to arrange your day so that most of your heavy appointments are scheduled for the morning. You don't want to be jousting with the toughest guy you know over some business deal two hours before you go on court. Plan to meet him earlier and give yourself time to recover.

Connors does not even like watching exciting movies during the afternoon if he has a match in the

70

evening. He feels it drains his energy level. He likes his energy all wound up like a coiled spring so that he can release all of it with maximum force where it matters most—on court.

If you operate best at a lower stress level, read, watch a movie, go for a jog or do some gentle limbering up exercises.

I came across a perfect example of that when I visited the Transamerica Open at the Cow Palace in San Francisco one year. Walking around the back of the stadium, I found Australian pro Kim Warwick wandering around with a grim look on his face and an unsheathed racquet in his hand. For a moment, I thought he was going to hit me over the head with it. In fact, he was psyching himself up for his first-round match against Arthur Ashe which was due to start about 20 minutes later.

By thinking about the match and avoiding the locker room banter which so often acts as a release from tension, Warwick was ensuring that he would walk on court at his best tension level. He was allowing nothing to distract him. He was ready.

"I'm so wound up for this one, I'll be three feet out of the starting blocks before they blow the whistle," the normally jocular Aussie told me. That night, Warwick played one of the best matches of his life to beat a top-form Ashe in three sets. Warwick, who so often has trouble getting "up" for his matches, had precisely the right tension pitch.

How to seek a lower stress level. If you operate best at a lower stress level, find some simple productive things to do during the two or three hours before your match. Read, watch a movie, go for a jog or do some gentle limbering up exercises. Ashe, who performs best at low tension, often spends his pre-match hours at tournaments doing a crossword puzzle. It takes his mind off the match and relaxes him down to his best level of tension.

There is no shortage of ways in which a player can calm pre-match nerves, and some can be a little bizarre. One leading European star, who has always had a problem ridding himself of excess energy, is not

**Going to the lavatory
before your match is also
a great relaxer.**

beyond finding a girl to spend some intimate hours with during the afternoon before an evening match. I don't know how many times he has managed it, but I recall at least one occasion when its calming effect helped him win a match in the Masters.

Of course, there are more conventional ways of reducing tension to a level that a person feels suits him best. Often, that's done subconsciously. Any regular members of the pro tour can tell as soon as they walk into the locker room just how far away Eddie Dibbs is from his match. The louder his voice and the more outrageous his jokes, the nearer he is to going on court. Whether he is aware of it or not, Dibbs is letting off steam and, by doing it, is lowering his level of tension to a point that best suits his generally hyper personality.

Quite apart from the fact that it might save embarrassment later on, going to the lavatory before your match is also a great relaxer. No matter how nervous they may be, very few pros ever get caught short by unruly bowels—although Nastase had to excuse himself in the middle of a match against Bob Hewitt in the British Hardcourt Championships at Bournemouth a few years back. Since the locker rooms there are situated a good 100 yards from the main court, Nastase had to make his way as quickly as circumstances would allow up the long path to the clubhouse—followed every inch of the way by the prying eye of a BBC television camera! It made for theater of the absurd as only Nastase can perform it.

What can result from poor preparation. I was due to play Jon Douglas, an old Los Angeles buddy, in the Pennsylvania Grasscourt Championships some years ago. I had beaten him twice already that year on concrete and now we were to play on grass which was Douglas' worst surface. If he will forgive me, I thought the match was a lock. So I got myself involved in a two-hour chess game right beforehand.

There is nothing as brutal as chess. The game's all

72

ego. What do you say if you lose? "I had a bad day? I was just dumb, my head was off?" When I lose in tennis, I can comfort myself by claiming that the other guy was just too much animal for me. But in chess, it's all intellect. If you get beat, the other guy was smarter.

So I brutalized my mind through a two-hour marathon and, when I got on court to play Douglas, I felt physically weak. Worse than that, I found that I was so emotionally drained that I did not have the mental strength to concentrate for the length of time it would take to win the match. Inevitably, I lost. I had gone out there poorly prepared and had paid the price. Bad preparation begets bad results.

So even for someone seeking to lower their tension level, I strongly recommend that they cross chess off the list of possible activities.

As we have seen, tension can manifest itself in many forms and the ways of dealing with it are just as varied. But deal with it you must, for as soon as you allow it to run out of control, it will destroy even the most carefully devised pre-match routines.

CHAPTER 5.
HOW YOU
CAN SHARPEN
YOUR GAME

CONCENTRATION: THE KEY
TO CONTROLLING EMOTIONS

It is said that necessity is the mother of invention. Back in 1961 I had a problem that necessitated some drastic action if I was to retain my sanity, preserve my self-respect and prevent myself from murdering my best friend.

My best friend, Larry Nagler, was at the core of my problem, and it is important to examine the effect he had on my mental state when he arrived at UCLA.

I had been top dog on the tennis team the year before he showed up. I rarely lost to a lesser ranked player. I had never failed to reach the final of any college tournament in which I had played and had, in fact, lost only one match, to Norm Perry, that whole year. I worked fanatically at my game, honing down my weaknesses and trying to add new shots to my armory. But most of all, I used my speed to outrun and outmaneuver my opponents.

Then Nagler arrived. To this day, I think he was one of the best athletes I have ever seen play the game. His physical prowess quickly earned him a place on the first string of the UCLA basketball team, and on a tennis court he was dynamite. He had this blinding speed which took me aback. I wasn't used to coming up against someone quicker than I was. The dreadful realization that I couldn't outrun him came as a shock. No matter what kind of trouble I put him in, no matter how fast I moved, Nagler was always able to move faster. It was bewildering and painful. I felt like a boxer flattened by a counter-punch seconds after he had landed his best right hook on his opponent's jaw.

For the whole of 1960, I didn't know what to do about him. By the middle of the following year, he had beaten me in six tournaments, including the National Clay Court Championships and the finals of three major intercollegiate tournaments. At the start, the matches were close. But then they got less close.

He was pervading my mind. I cringed with fear when I walked out on court against him. His ever-increasing dominance brought out all my insecurities. Instead of focusing on my strengths and his weaknesses, I did just the opposite. I became obsessed with the fact that he was too quick for me.

All the luck seemed to flow on his side of the court, although, in fact, he often forced luck to run with him by trying so hard for every ball. But, on occasions, the incredible things that happened were enough to numb my brain. I remember one point in particular that drove me to the outer edges of sanity. We were in the semifinals of an invitational tournament in Balboa. Having split the first two sets, we were deep into the third. On a crucial point, I had worked him off the court on his forehand side, hit what felt like a sure winner deep to his backhand corner and, for good measure, followed it to the net. As usual, Nagler made a superhuman effort to reach the ball and managed to throw back a desperate, but hopelessly short, lob. I waited confidently at the net. Only one of two things could happen, I thought— either it would fall short of the net or just clear it. In the event of the latter, I would have the sitter of all sitters to bang away to any part of the court I chose.

But, of course, there was a third possibility—a

thousand to one outside chance—and to my horror and disbelief, it happened. The lob landed smack on top of the tape, rolled gently onto my side of the net and died. I stood there dumbfounded for a second. "How could this be?" I asked myself. "Why must I be plagued by this person? Isn't it bad enough that he is the fastest man on earth—must he also be the luckiest?"

In the finals of the Southern California Intercollegiate Championships at the Valley Hunt Club, his rabbit's foot was again at work. He won the first set, but I had a chance to go ahead by a service break late in the second. Nagler was at net and I hit a quick, offensive lob which caught him by surprise as he moved forward. It was tantalizingly low. In desperation, he made a mighty leap for it, swung and missed it completely. A slight smile began to play across my lips. But I was jumping to conclusions. As I looked on like a spectator, he wheeled around, chased the ball down from behind and tossed back a high lob. I had to start the point over and eventually lost it. The incident only compounded my insecurities and he had little further difficulty in closing out the set—and the match.

Step by step, I reached the stage where physical paralysis would set in when I played him. He was starting to transfix me. Although he had certain limitations to his game, he wouldn't bother working on his weaknesses, like I did. He would simply barrel his way through to still more success by utilizing his strengths. This attitude only served to worsen my psychological trauma so that even his weak shots started to be too much for me.

For instance, he had limitations with his passing shots. He couldn't put topspin on his backhand, so whenever he had to run wide or short on that side, he would try to slice the ball down the line. I would be sitting on the net, totally aware of what he was going to do but, despite my usual quickness, I was quite unable to reach the ball in time. My legs simply refused to move. Obviously, I was in deep trouble.

76

Toward the end of that year, he had got me into such a state that I had no judgment left. I started to imagine his shots were going out. Five or six times in a match, I would let balls go that would land feet inside the baseline. Afraid to play my shots, I was just willing his to go out. I was no longer rational.

Worse than that, I was starting to hate Larry Nagler, who, as I have said, was the best friend I had on campus. I told the UCLA coach, J.D. Morgan, that I didn't want to practice with Larry anymore. Every time we played, I just became aggravated. As my insecurity grew, I became oversensitized to his behavior. He appeared to have become very cocky and smug. I imagined that there was something demeaning in his manner and that he looked forward to playing me because winning had become so easy.

As these feelings grew, the problem worsened. I really don't know what might have happened if I had not hit on the solution which enabled me to break the spell and get back on an even keel.

It all came to a head in the 1961 Southern California Intercollegiate tournament. I had defeated the late Rafael Osuna in the semifinals, and Larry and I were in the locker room at the Valley Hunt Club changing for the final. It was to be the seventh time we had met in tournaments since the beginning of the previous summer and I had not won once. Larry passed some remark, probably quite lighthearted, which I interpreted as cocky and demeaning. It triggered all my black thoughts about his condescending attitude toward me, and something snapped. I almost went for his throat. Fortunately, I grabbed hold of myself before the scene turned into a ridiculous brawl and went off into a corner by myself to calm down.

How the tide finally turns. I knew I had to do something about this and, as we walked out on court, I was still struggling with a solution. Between the locker room and the court I hit on it: I would force Nagler right out of my mind. I would fix my thoughts on one

Between the locker room and the court I hit on it: I would fix my thoughts on one fundamental and simple idea, like, "Watch the ball."

fundamental and simple idea, like, "Watch the ball." This would fill my mind, and nothing else would be able to work its way into my conscious thought pattern. There would be no room. To increase my focus and cut out distraction, I would never look at Nagler. I would simply stare down at the ground between points and keep repeating out loud, "Watch the ball. Concentrate!"

And it worked. I beat him 6–1, 6–1.

That type of intense concentration has been used independently by many players—Fred Stolle made three consecutive Wimbledon finals as soon as he adopted the "stare-at-the-feet" routine—although, at the time, it was not part of the average tennis instruction manual. But it worked for me at that crisis point in my career and it has worked for me ever since.

I don't always say exactly the same things to myself, but they are always short and simple. The idea is to *focus on some helpful fundamental.*

For instance, I tend to become conservative when I get ahead in a match. So, at this stage, I start repeating, "Attack. Concentrate!" This seems to give my body some forward impetus as I hit and causes my shot to retain its pace.

When returning a fast serve, I have found I have a tendency not to follow the ball closely enough. Often under these circumstances, I key in on the phrase, "Watch it bounce. Concentrate!" If I make sure to focus on the ball as it hits the ground, I make cleaner contact with my service return.

The possibilities are endless and differ from player to player, but the strategy is always the same. Pick something that is useful to your game and concentrate on it. It shouldn't be too complex or involved like, "Follow through six inches above your left shoulder blade." That should be left for the practice court. Keep it simple and it will work.

The concept is much like the one employed in Transcendental Meditation. The person sits in a room

78

with as little outside stimulation as possible and re-
peats a nonsense syllable, called a "mantra," over and
over again, while concentrating on it. This fills the
mind with a simple, unitary thought. Since only one
thought can occupy your conscious mind at a time, the
welter of worrisome and anxiety-provoking thoughts
which might ordinarily be there are thrust out. For a
time, at least, your mind finds relief from the fears and
tensions of everyday living. Users of this technique
claim that it is very relaxing. In fact, the concept seems
to receive backup from the eminent psychologist,
Gustav Jung, who noted early in this century that
calculated, rational thought serves to suppress
emotion.

And suppressing emotion was exactly what I had
to do, if I was ever going to give myself a chance of
beating Nagler. But you may wonder how, if you fill
your conscious mind with only one simple, repetitious
thought, you will be able to make those thousands of
split-second tactical decisions that are necessary to
playing proper tennis?

The answer lies in the nature of the physical interaction between mind and body. The system works like
a sophisticated computer-driven machine. Our minds
operate in the same way computers do, programmed
with responses to fit each situation. The information
received by the mind is transmitted to the body, which
immediately acts on its instructions. If the computer
has been programmed properly to begin with and
there is no interference with the processing and trans-
mitting of information, the response will be correct.

But strong, uncontrolled emotion throws a mon-
key wrench into the system. Keeping your pulse rate
under reasonable control is essential if the messages
from the brain are to arrive in a coherent and de-
cipherable state. When someone functions well in a
crisis, it often means that his computer has been well-
programmed and is relaying a series of rational and
organized messages to the body. In many situations,

including tennis matches, there is simply not enough time to figure out what to do by rational analysis. The proper responses have to be worked out in advance.

If I were not entirely convinced of this after the match against Nagler at Valley Hunt, I was left in no doubt as to its validity after a much more serious incident several years later. Then it really was a matter of life and death. I was at the controls of a light aircraft with the self-same Larry Nagler at my side and another close friend, George Zwerdling, in the back. We had taken a trip to Rio de Janeiro in a single engine Bellanca and, on our return, were overflying a stretch of Bolivian jungle. Without warning, the engine suddenly quit.

It was every pilot's nightmare-turned-reality. Yet, strangely enough, I did not feel any great fear or emotional stress. Although I was quite unaware of it at the time, Nagler tells me I spoke out loud to myself throughout the descent. Apparently, I was saying in a mechanical, rote way, things like, "Slow it down to 100 . . . feather the prop . . . electrical switches off . . . ."

In other words, my computer had turned onto automatic. Because I was concentrating so intensely on the task at hand, which was pressing, to say the least, and because my brain had been drilled over and over again with the emergency checklist, there was no room for the kind of emotions that would normally surface when one is gliding the depths of a tropical forest. I gathered later that Nagler and Zwerdling, unhindered by the demands of controlling an airplane, had plenty of time to experience a variety of emotions.

My own moment of fear began only after we had made first contact with the ground and were careening out of control along a dry riverbed. At that stage, there was nothing more I could do, and, with no task to focus on, normal emotions erupted. It was only by chance that all of three of us were helicoptered out with our skins relatively intact.

INSTINCT: EVERY PLAYER'S ASSET

During a tennis match, the computer in your brain can work independently on two completely different levels. One is the studied and conscious effort to monitor your match strategy and keep your emotions and concentration intact, which we've just discussed; the other is the subconscious, split-second instinctive level during the course of a point.

As it is important to understand the differences and the details of these two functions, let's now examine the instinctive level in depth so you get a clearer picture of precisely what takes place mentally when two players strike a ball between them on a tennis court.

Learning by reward and punishment. Once the ball is in play, there is no time to think at a conscious level. What occurs after the serve is struck is achieved by what people commonly call "instinct." But what is "instinct"? Basically, it is a complex calculation being made at a level of the nervous system below voluntary, conscious thought.

It is a sequence of reactions to a set of cues that we have learned by a long process of rewards and punishments. You hit your forehand passing shot high down the line against an opponent with a good backhand volley and he bangs away an easy crosscourt winner. You have been punished. Next time you go low crosscourt to his weaker forehand volley and he dumps it into the net. You have been rewarded.

What emerges after a time is a vast array of probable successes and failures which are stored in the subconscious and come to light with each corresponding court situation and response. One of the major differences between the great player and the lesser one is the speed at which the tennis brain reacts with the correct probabilities coupled with his ability to use these unfailingly by "instinct" when required.

The fact that he invariably seems to play the correct shot is one of the main reasons why John McEnroe

81

> **Instinct is a complex calculation made at a level of the nervous system below voluntary, conscious thought.**

has risen so fast. Obviously, he only needed to be rewarded or punished a few times before the computer in his brain was able to give him the right answers. Most of us take much longer, but that is no reason for despair.

To take just two examples, the New Zealander Onny Parun and Bob Carmichael of Australia both spent several years in the lower echelons of the pro game learning to program limited ability to a level that would enable them to compete with—and sometimes beat—the best in the world. By their late 20's, both had proved that hard work pays off. Parun was ranked 25th in the world for over a year on the ATP computer, and Carmichael was good enough to beat Ken Rosewall and become a Wimbledon quarterfinalist.

When you stop to consider the computation required to hit a tennis ball accurately, it becomes very clear why Parun and Carmichael are two very normal guys blessed with an unusual amount of endurance, patience and drive, while McEnroe is the kind of genius who comes along not more than two or three times in a decade.

To continue with our two hard-working friends, let us say that Parun is at the net waiting for Carmichael's return from the baseline. Based on his past knowledge of Carmichael's game and a multitude of minute cues in the position of the body as he begins his stroke, Parun starts to move to his left, in anticipation of a forehand hit down the line to his own backhand volley.

As he begins his move, Parun will have already estimated the approximate amount of power with which Carmichael will hit the ball and whether he will have time to go forward into the volley or will have to be content with a blocked return.

Then, the instant the ball is in flight between Carmichael's racquet and his own, Parun's computer will be taking into account trajectory, speed, wind, spin and angle. This information will enable him to fine-tune the angle of his lateral move so that he can

82

intercept this spinning, flying object as closely to the net as possible.

Further, Parun's computer will simultaneously be sifting through a vast number of possibilities to determine where and how hard his own shot should be hit. He will take into account his own capabilities with a backhand volley as well as Carmichael's ability to reach different areas of the court from his current position within a given time.

Which shot will give him the best overall chance of winning the point? Is that the shot that Carmichael will find most difficult to handle or the shot that carries the least likelihood of error? Somewhere a balance must be struck so that the combined probabilities of winning the point reach a maximum. The variables are endless . . . the decision irrevocable.

Can you imagine the hours it would take to sit down with paper and pencil and work out all those computations (ball traveling at 52 m.p.h. over a distance of 24 feet with error probability .237 in wind gusting to . . . ?) Yet a top player can make the right calculation time and again with a margin of error no wider than a gnat's eyelash—and all in a matter of microseconds.

Obviously, the conscious brain is not capable of such a feat. But equally it does not happen by magic. The muscles do not move by themselves. That is where the programming comes in. As soon as the correct set of answers to a whole host of varied and complicated problems is stored, you will be able to play tennis like Ken Rosewall or John McEnroe.

Instinct vs. intelligence. People call Rosewall and McEnroe "intelligent" tennis players, Pancho Segura likewise. But it is not necessarily correct. Intelligence implies a conscious thought process which solves a particular problem. When Segura wrong-footed an opponent and left him stumbling around like a fool, people would tap their heads, smile knowingly and say to each other, "intelligent." But Pancho wasn't, at that precise moment, being "intelligent." He was playing by instinct. Now if he had studied his opponent and thought out all those moves prior to practicing them over and over again until they were programmed and became instinctive, then "intelligent" would have been a justifiable description of his talents (and with Segura this may have been the case). But with other players, it is possible to drill the reward-punishment sequence into them until the computer produces the right answers. These then become instinctive tennis players, not necessarily intelligent ones.

There are situations in which projecting intelligence and planning, rather than instinct, result in disaster. And even in instances where the plans are simple and basically sound, they often go awry. Charlie Pasarell provided an excellent example of this in a tournament in Buenos Aires. He was playing the deceptively talented Indian champion, Ramanathan Krishnan, and stood at match point down on his own serve.

As Pasarell later related, "I had it all figured out. I thought, on this one I'm going to fool him. I'll kick in a high one on his backhand, sneak into the net and knock off the volley before he knows what happened.

"So I threw in a wide serve, came in and had an easy backhand volley. But I underspun it too much and it sat up in the middle of the court. It gave him an easy forehand. He had been catching me all day with the short crosscourt, so I moved to my right. But he lobbed down the line. Things were not working out too well. I turned and ran after it as fast as I could. I barely got it and as I threw up a short lob, I tripped. He saw me on the ground and hit the ball easy crosscourt. I know Krish didn't think I could get it. But I jumped up, grabbed my racquet and, with the wrong grip, shoveled one down the line for a winner."

Not exactly the way Pasarell had planned it. But few points will respond to precise planning. Too many things can go wrong.

Don't overload your computer. The greater the talent and array of strokes a player possesses, the more complex his computer system needs to be. If a player can *only* go crosscourt with his backhand, this limitation makes a whole area of possible calculations redundant. However, if you are Arthur Ashe or Lew Hoad, with more shots in your repertoire than bullets in a machine gun, your computer can sometimes get overloaded with the sheer variety of calculations that must be made.

It was therefore not uncommon to see Hoad, who ruled Wimbledon and much of the tennis world in the mid-50's, make a terrible hash of a seemingly easy shot because his computer was still sorting out whether to use the topspin lob, the flat-hit backhand crosscourt or the down-the-line slice. Hoad sometimes suffered from an embarrassment of riches.

Several years ago, I injured my right shoulder. It became increasingly bothersome with use, so I decided to rest it for a time by playing left-handed. At the start, I was incredibly weak and able only to bloop the ball down the middle of the court. I had no decisions to make whatsoever since there was only one thing I could do with the ball. But against lower-level players, this turned out to be very effective. While they were worrying about coming in or staying back, drop shotting or hitting deep, topspinning or slicing, I just put my head down, ran like mad and pushed the ball down the middle. It drove them crazy. Sometimes it is useful to have no alternatives.

No cues cause problems, too. In addition to overloading the human computer, another way to confuse it is to remove one of the basic signals or cues from which it reads its information. Although most of the information is visual, much of it comes from sources that are quite subtle, such as determining wind velocity from sensations on the skin. Even the ear is a transmitter of these cues and it requires some reprogramming of the computer to be able to play well without

One of the basic
ingredients of greatness
is how quickly a player is
able to act on a very
limited number of cues.

the benefit of sound.

This was one of the reasons why so many players had difficulty when the so-called spaghetti double-string racquet was introduced briefly in Europe and at the U.S. Open in 1977. After Stan Smith lost to Mike Fishbach, one of the spaghetti merchants, in an early round at Forest Hills, Smith complained of not being able to hear the ball come off Fishbach's loosely strung racquet.

"It threw my timing off completely," Smith admitted afterward. "It's amazing how one gets to rely on sound without realizing it."

Like any good player, Smith would have adapted pretty quickly had the double-string not been outlawed by the International Tennis Federation (ITF). But the incident provided a good example of how reprogramming is required when new elements are introduced into a complex pattern of play.

Under normal circumstances, the cues available to a player on a tennis court are too numerous, too varied and too miniscule to be sifted through the conscious mind. Like the Indian tracker able to follow a trail over bare rock, it is the hallmark of a great tennis player to be able to pick up pieces of information in his opponent's game that no one else can see.

One of the basic ingredients of greatness is how quickly a player is able to act on a very limited number of cues. To explain this better, let's take it in stages.

The basic idea is to know where you have to run to meet the ball after your opponent has hit it. The elementary player will just wait to see where the ball bounces and then try to run after it. The better player will pick up the trajectory and speed of the ball in flight and—subconsciously, through his computer—calculate where it will land.

But the top players don't wait as long as that. They soon become aware of any pattern in their opponent's shot selection. This gives them some idea of where the ball will go, even before the actual stroke begins. Then they watch their opponent's body and deduce from the way he shapes up to the ball where he is going to hit it.

Players who are able to pick up these cues exceptionally early often look a great deal faster than they are because they give themselves a head start. Ken Rosewall was the ultimate master in this respect. He was always pretty quick, but the superb tracking of his computer made him seem faster than light. Opponents were continually bemused and frustrated by his ability to simply appear at the precise spot where they had hit the ball. Contrary to popular belief, Rosewall did not have Mercury's wings on his heels. But he did—and still does—possess a highly sophisticated tennis computer that reads an opponent's intentions within a split second of that player deciding what he intends to do.

Obviously, the great players also get pretty good at disguising their shots. Arthur Ashe is one of the most adept in this respect. By dragging the wrist and snapping it at the moment of impact, Ashe makes it almost impossible to detect where he is aiming. I always found him a frustrating opponent, not merely because of this ability, but because there was never any pattern to his thought process. He always seemed to come up with a random selection of shots, many of which left you standing, like an idiot, at the wrong side of the court.

More conventional players usually play to a pattern and it is often profitable to get into a guessing game with them and try to work in sync with their minds. At club level this should be possible once you have played someone a couple of times. Almost all players are much more comfortable doing certain things under certain conditions, and it should not take an average competent player long to link his own computer into that of his opponent.

Many of the seemingly incongruous results in pro tennis originate from one player being unable to read the other man's shots. This was the reason behind Marty Riessen's suprisingly good record against Rod

More conventional players usually play to a pattern and it is often profitable to try to work in sync with their minds.

Laver when they were both playing the World Championship Tennis (WCT) circuit in the early 70's. Laver's overall record put him a class above Riessen, but you would never have known it when they met head-to-head. Riessen beat the Rocket as frequently as he lost to him, and after their matches Laver would often shake his head and say, "I don't know what it is about Marty. I just don't seem to be able to pick his shots." Rosewall, on the other hand, read Riessen like a book, and it was years before Riessen even came close to beating him.

While much of what happens during a tennis match takes place at a subconscious level—not unlike driving a car—on another mental plane, the player is watching the match develop and making conscious adjustments. For example, if your opponent's backhand is weak, you may make a point of noting this fact. As soon as you have done so, it will automatically be programmed into your future calculations. Without thinking, your computer will be adjusted and, from then on, a higher percentage of your shots will find their way to his weak backhand.

Basically, your conscious mind changes the program, and the computer does the rest. But you should be careful not to make the changes too quickly or too drastically.

BELIEVE IN YOUR GAME PLAN
I read somewhere that you should always change a losing game and never change a winning one. That sounds obvious. As with most overly simplified nostrums, it is easier to repeat than to enact.

For instance, how do you know that the game you are playing is, in fact, a losing game? I suppose you could wait until you lose. Even then you could not be sure. Maybe the problem was in the execution rather than the strategy. Maybe your opponent was just better than you and would have beaten you even more badly with some other strategy.

The problem is twofold. One is to know how far

behind you must get with a particular strategy before you become convinced it is a losing one and abandon it; the second is then to choose an alternative which gives you a better chance of winning.

Consider an imaginary match between two members of my Pepperdine team, Leo Palin and Craig Edwards, who have totally different styles. Palin, a Finn, has solid European ground strokes, while Edwards is a typical American serve-and-volley player who is less certain off the ground. As we look in on the match, they are deep in the first set and the score is even. Edwards has been attacking at the net every chance he gets and Palin has been defending on the baseline. Now Palin starts to get the upper hand; he passes Edwards several times. Edwards misses a volley or two and loses his serve and the set. He quickly falls behind in the second. He is missing volleys and Palin starts to look confident, hitting more good passing shots. Edwards now approaches the net with trepidation, fearing that Palin has figured out his game and knows how to handle him.

What should he do? Edwards decides to stay back and play Palin from the baseline for a while, hoping to throw him off with his new tactics. In this way, he hopes to regain his own confidence and change a game which appears to be heading for defeat.

Edwards has just made the inexperienced player's typical mistake. He has allowed a few good shots by his opponent and a few of his own errors to convince him to abandon his normal style of play. Now he will be matching his own weak ground strokes directly against Palin's strong ones—which is exactly what Palin wants.

The real problem was not Palin's passing shots. He only hit a few of them. Nor was it Edwards' volley. It was Edwards' fear and loss of purpose. Once he began to worry about his game and think about strategy changes, he was in trouble. Of course his volley deteriorated. How could he concentrate with a clear mind and full-bloodedly press home his volleying attack, while he was wondering if he wouldn't be better off on the baseline?

Think about Palin's position. Could he have been as confident as he looked? Unlikely. All of us have put together a few fine shots and taken a small lead, only to have our touch evaporate a few games later—and with it our lead. We all know how tenuous those hot streaks are and how difficult it is to keep hitting good shots against a determined opponent.

Play with purpose and consistency. Most successful players have one thing in common in their approach to a match and that is purpose. They realize that matches have many temporary ebbs and flows. They are not shaken by these. They are not blown from course by the first wind. They plan a solid strategy based on a reasonable assessment of their own and their opponent's strengths and weaknesses and never think of running for cover at the first sign of trouble. They usually play with intensity and purpose until their opponent cracks. If they have misjudged him they make him prove it. Their opponent is forced to show his hand.

All this does not mean that one should never deviate from one's initial game plan. Deviations are often necessary. But in my experience, the vast majority of errors are made by players changing too soon and too much, rather than too late and too little. The improper changes are made through fear and lack of confidence. The proper ones are made with a cool head and usually are not drastic. It is sometimes better to play a match with a bad game plan, providing you do so with strength and determination, rather than to vacillate and flounder around with no game plan at all.

The professionals have been through the brief fluctuations that occur during a match hundreds of times. But they don't let it phase them. The top pros, especially, are very stable.

None more so than Chris Evert. She is not blessed with Martina Navratilova's strength, Virginia Wade's serve or Evonne Goolagong's overall physical prowess. But she is without peer in concentration and mental stability. She never wavers.

Most successful players will play with intensity and purpose until their opponents crack.

A talented opponent may throw her full range of superior physical resources at Evert, but she doesn't blink. Even if she gets behind to a serve-and-volley player, she will not fall for the temptation of changing her game to meet a temporary crisis. She just assumes that her "grind-em-up-from-the-baseline" style of play is the strongest game she has and that, sooner or later, her opponent will crumble. She is usually right.

Rod Laver's style was the exact opposite of Evert's but he shared her philosophy. He refused to temper his shots, regardless of the score. He often summarized his strategy by saying, "I just keep hitting them hard until they go in." Ditto for Connors and Borg.

Again, I must emphasize that this is *usually* the case, but not always. It depends partially on how balanced a player's game is. If he is equally at home on the baseline or at the net, then he has more options than a pure baseliner or volleyer. After all, what is Solomon to do if he is being beaten from the baseline? Rush the net? McEnroe, however, can serve and volley, play steady on the baseline or do half a dozen other things with equal facility.

But at times, even the pros miscalculate their ability to adapt and change their games. A good example occurred in the finals of the American Airlines Tennis Games at Palm Springs in 1976. Jimmy Connors somehow intimidated Roscoe Tanner into staying on the baseline and trading ground strokes. Roscoe usually follows his bullet serve into the net and pounds winners with his volley. His power, coupled with the pressure of his net attack, cover up for the lack of flexibility in his movements and strokes. Instead, he elected to maneuver around helplessly on the baseline with Connors, a guy who is as quick as a cat and probably possesses the best ground strokes in the world. Tanner had let a few passing shots from Connors convince him that his own strengths were not good enough. So he discarded them and tried to play Connors at his own game. The consequences were inevitable. But Tanner learned his lesson. A few months later, he reverted to his serve-and-volley game and crushed Connors in the Wimbledon quarterfinal.

Consistency is crucial, not only in pursuing your own strengths as a player, but also in bringing to fruition a style of concentrated percentage tennis—a style that wins most of the matches. I have never totally agreed with the long-standing adage that winning tennis matches basically revolves around winning the big points. The most important thing is to ensure that you *get* to the big points—and get there often. Then you just have to win your share. Granted, the truly great players—the Chris Everts, Jimmy Connors or Billie Jean Kings—win far more than their share. But for the rest, living up to one's potential as a player involves consistency. Day in and day out, tennis matches are not won by making big shots. They are won by getting the routine service returns in court, making the easy volley and hanging tough throughout the match. It is the losers who are always in trouble and trying to extricate themselves with streaks of brilliance. The players who make all those great shots and come off court wondering why they have lost need look no further for the answer than all those counterbalancing unforced errors.

It is much the same for the great pool players who rarely have to make the fancy shots of which they are capable. They think ahead, play the percentages and leave the balls in positions where the simple shot will do.

The professional tennis players also position themselves well and usually produce their most spectacular shots when under pressure. Although the club player may enjoy going for the big shot, the enjoyment that it brings tends to be temporary. The player who wants to win will cultivate the less spectacular aspects of the game and learn the lessons of:

Concentration—Focus your attention on a simple, helpful aspect of your game to keep unwanted thoughts and emotions at bay.

Instinct—Let your unconscious reactions feed the computer in your brain so you can sort out the probabilities of success or failure in a given situation.

Belief in your game plan—Strength of purpose and confidence in your abilities are essential to a sound, initial game plan; plus a commitment to percentage stroke play and sound positioning. If changes are necessary, adopt them only after cold analysis, not out of fear.

CHAPTER 6.
THE FEAR
OF LOSING

The heat inside the Rizal Stadium in Manila had reached suffocation point. Air, and other properties essential to human survival, seemed to be getting scarcer by the minute. What oxygen remained in the turgid atmosphere was rapidly being passed through the over-worked lungs of 7,000 enthusiastic Philippinos.

In a corner of the dimly lit stadium, John Newcombe, Ross Case and Geoff Masters were not helping the situation by laughing their heads off in between throwing out dubiously helpful comments to their mate, Colin Dibley.

Although painful, the comic aspects of the situation were undeniable. Dibley, a tall, angular Australian, was limping up and down the baseline, his right leg stiff as a ramrod with cramp, while at the other end of the court his fellow Aussie, Allan Stone, was desperately trying to close out a match he should have won several games before.

Stone had been advancing steadily to a 5–1 lead in the final set when Dibley felt the first twinges of the cramp that often affects him in hot climates. Now the match was in the tie breaker; seven match points had been squandered and Dibley's leg and Stone's mind had something in common—paralysis.

The pros have a name for Stone's mental anguish —choking. And by any standards, this was destined to be a choke to remember.

"I could see Allan was having trouble concentrating and, of course, I knew he was inclined to get nervous in situations like that, so I thought I might as well give it a go," said Dibley. "Getting cramps was bad enough. There was no point in going through all that pain and losing. I reckoned winning would make it all a bit more worthwhile."

So, hobbling as he was, Dibley kept on winning points by the simple method of standing there and whacking the ball. Stone, preoccupied by this time with the basic problem of trying to get the ball over the net, seemed transfixed by the crippled figure in front of him and completely failed to steer the ball out of Dibley's reach.

After the first few points of the tie breaker, Stone was in worse shape than Dibley. The memory of seven match points missed against a man who could barely walk, let alone run, haunted him with every passing minute and the problem of his own physical fatigue could not be discounted. The Philippino crowd, who had never seen anything like it, screeched with delight; the other Aussie players were doubled up with mirth in the corner as dust from the dry dirt court clogged their nostrils.

"By that stage I knew I had a chance," said Dibley. "Mostly I was just hitting my first serve as hard as I could and hoping he'd miss the return, because there was no way I could get to the net. But when I finally got to match point, I managed to hobble up there and stick over a volley. Poor Allan. I don't think he could believe it."

Back at the hotel, it took the houseboy a couple of hours to help Dibley unknot his muscles. But despite a few beers that night, the damage to Stone's confidence was probably more lasting. He couldn't win the match in Manila because he became afraid and that fear made him play a tentative game.

But why should players become nervous before or during a tennis match? What can happen that is so frightening? You can't get hurt. It is easy to understand why you should be nervous before a bullfight when you might get gored in the stomach, or before a boxing match when you might get your nose smashed to pulp. But a tennis match?

TESTING YOUR MIND AND OVERCOMING INFERIORITY

The reason any true competitor is in a high state of tension before walking on court centers on the fact that a tennis match is a test—a mental test, which in tennis is where you are most vulnerable—in the mind. The physical aspect is less of a problem. If you lose because you are not fit enough, there is a simple and obvious solution: Get out and train harder. If you lose because the other guy or girl is stronger and hits the ball too hard for you, tough luck. It's a fact of life and you can't do much about it.

But if you flunk the mental test, if you are not tough enough on the big points, if your resolve collapses when match point looms, then it is your self-image that takes the punishment. Your worst fears are realized. Your character is flawed. You are a "loser." And that is frightening. There is nowhere to hide. If you end up losing a match you could have won through an inability to handle the pressure, your inferiority is clearly displayed. The fear of having to face that inferiority is what causes the tension. Why?

In our society, mental ability is more important than physical ability. There is no stigma attached to physical illness. Mental illness is a different matter. It is easier to say, "Excuse me, I'm lame," than, "Excuse me, I'm dumb."

Human beings are elevated above the other species because of their mental capability. It is not degrading to be outrun by your German shepherd. But outsmarted by him? That's quite another matter. We

96

are willing to concede our physical inferiorities. But it is largely upon our mental abilities that the fragile structure of the human ego is bolstered and sustained.

This explanation of the fear involved in winning or losing tennis matches evolves, in some degree, from the works of Alfred Adler, which we described in Chapter 2. Basically, he felt that our dominant drive was for power and superiority—a drive fueled by the need to escape from deep-seated feelings of inferiority.

Relating this to tennis matches, one can see how winning or losing becomes a test of inferiority. Every time a person loses, those feelings of inferiority are reinforced. The result proves it; you just lost. Argue your way out of that one!

Part of the elation one feels from winning is based on the satisfaction derived from knowing that you are superior to someone, at least on that particular day.

Proving that superiority creates a lot of tension. Whether you want to admit it or not, the chance to prove that superiority is very important to you. There are not many opportunities during the course of a normal week in which you have such a clear-cut test of whether you are inferior or superior to somebody as when you walk on a tennis court.

Tennis is a test, the passing or failing of which cannot be hidden. In other areas of endeavor results can be obscured. In business, for example, there is often no clear-cut winner or loser. Business results are not generally unitary events. They are an accumulation of the results of many small decisions made over a period of time. It is usually not clear which decision was responsible for which result. Moreover, the world at large does not really know what is happening on a day-to-day basis. How well or how badly is business going for Michael, the young fellow who works for the insurance company downtown? He looks well dressed, lives in a nice house and always has enough money to buy tennis balls. But maybe his boss considers him an incompetent. The outside world will

> Part of the elation one feels from winning is based on the satisfaction derived from knowing that you are superior to someone, at least on that particular day.

97

probably never know. The amount of money you make is the way you keep score in business, just as match results are in tennis. But how many people would like to publish a copy of their financial statements? Not many. It is a very sensitive area and most people are afraid they are not doing well enough. I used to think nobody told anyone how much money he was making because of the IRS or something. But it's not so. The subject is taboo because of the loss of self-esteem involved if one is making too little. In tennis you have no choice; after a loss the word is out, whether you like it or not.

The inevitability of having to face up to the result of the test and the risk that you might fail is what causes the fear. It affects all players, great and much less great, highly strung or outwardly serene. Few champions have displayed a more commanding or serene presence on court than Stan Smith. When he was Wimbledon champion and ranked No. 1 in the world in 1971, opponents used to find him awesomely self-confident. When I spoke to him recently, I asked him if he used to get nervous during this supremely successful period of his career. "Sure I got nervous," he replied, "most often when I was ahead and close to finishing off a tough opponent."

Finishing off your opponent *is* **frightening.** I found that a large majority of top players expressed similar sentiments. It was finishing off a set or a match that created the most anxiety. Being match point up is much more nerve-racking than being match point down. But that does not seem to make sense. Why should you be frightened just as you close in for the kill? You should be *more* frightened when your opponent is closing in on you. After all, when you are up match point, you can afford to lose a few points or games. You will still only be back to even and can win the match from there. But if you are down match point and lose it, there is no return.

I know from my own experience of competing

against the world's best players like Ashe, Laver or Newcombe that there is nothing that turns your racquet arm into jelly quicker than reaching match point after a long, close struggle. I prefer not to remember the number of times I have failed to clear the net with my service return when I have been match point up. I had the feeling that I had to finish my opponent off immediately, lest he wiggle free and I never see match point again. Contrastingly, when I was match point down, I felt looser and was almost always able to put the ball in play. I rarely made mistakes at that stage. Why? Because by the time my opponent had reached match point, I had already, to a large extent, emotionally accepted defeat. This did not mean that I did not fight on to the limit of my capabilities. I did, and in many respects, fought better than at any other time in the match. But in my own mind, I had very little to lose and quite a bit to gain. If I won, I was a hero, having, by sheer courage and other indefinable qualities, managed to tear the match out of the hands of my opponent. I had a certain emotional numbness to pain and a feeling of unreality at this stage. Only if I were able to win the point and perhaps draw even would my nerves return to life. Suddenly, I would be back in the match, with victory again within my grasp and the pressure on.

Much of this has to do with the superbly conceived structure of the tennis scoring system which I will discuss shortly but, more important, the fact of being nervous when you hold match point revolves around the test problem again. At this stage, you have cornered yourself. By arriving within one point of victory, you have proved that you are capable of winning the match. Now you must do it.

If you are playing Jimmy Connors or Chris Evert and you are not in the world's Top 10, you will be up against a player with superior skill—better strokes and wider experience. When you lose, you will be able to rationalize, quite correctly, that you were beaten by an expert player and that it was no contest.

Being nervous when you hold match point revolves around the test problem again. By arriving within one point of victory, you have proved you are capable of winning the match. Now you must do it.

The chances are that you will not have been very nervous because you had practically no hope of overcoming your pre-established position of inferiority. There really was no mental test. However, if you actually get to match pont—even against a Connors or an Evert—you will have proved, no matter how unlikely it may seem, that you were *physically* capable of winning. By reaching match point, there can be no argument about your being as good, if not better, than your opponent, regardless of name or fame, on that particular day. But if, having reached match point, you cannot clinch the victory, you will have failed the mental test. You will have demonstrated for all the world to see that you had your opponent down and didn't have the courage to finish him off.

The scoring system adds to stress. The unique scoring system in tennis—a brilliantly devised series of independent battles fought for games and sets— makes the test even tougher. To win a game in tennis you must win a minimum of four points, and it doesn't matter whether you are 6–0, 5–0 up or 0–6, 0–5 down. Each game is an independent contest. Although four points may not seem like much at first, against a tough opponent who is determined to make a stand for a particular game, four points is a long way away. It is like house-to-house fighting in a war. Even though you may have superior forces, each house must be fought for and taken individually. A tenacious opponent can make you suffer for each one. And if you should lose momentum, he can, starting at any time, take them all back.

In basketball, football or soccer, any team that establishes a substantial lead has the option of closing the game up, playing safe and letting the clock do the rest. As long as they do not make any stupid mistakes, the simple passage of time will eventually finish off their opponents. They don't actually have to do the winning themselves. Having occupied one position they can sit tight, adopt a defensive strategy and wait.

But in tennis, time is irrelevant. The match will go on and if you do not take the points, your opponent will. And therein lies the beauty and the inherent terror of the tennis scoring system. No matter how big your lead, you are never safe.

In tennis, where each game is independent, the margin is never more than three points before a player can afford to lose one point.

Even in table tennis, where time is also irrelevant, the scoring system is such that anyone establishing a 20–3 lead is virtually certain of victory, because all he has to do is win one more point out of the next 17. The person who is behind cannot afford to lose *one* point. But in tennis, where each game is independent, the margin is never more than three points before a player can afford to lose one point. In fact, once he is even, he can lose as many as he likes, as long as he doesn't get behind by two. And once the player who is behind starts winning games, he will have sown the seeds of frustration, annoyance and maybe just a twinge of fear into his opponent.

When you are in position to close out a match, the greatest danger is that you will change your game out of fear and the anxiety that your opponent will somehow wiggle free. The usual problem is becoming tentative and playing the match as though it were a football game in which you could simply stall and run out the clock. You can only win by continuing to move forward at your own pace, to continue winning the points. But you must stick to your own style. Hitting out blindly for winners in a panic-stricken attempt to force victory is as bad as pooping the ball back and praying that your opponent will miss. Don't let fear induce you to change a winning game.

To use another analogy, the climax to a tennis match is similar to a bullfight. You have to play the part of the matador. As long as the bull is still on his feet, he is dangerous, just as the man across the net is dangerous until you have won match point. And the moment of truth—the instant when you must go in over the horns with your sword—is the most dangerous and frightening time of all. But there is no way out. The bull will not go down unless you kill him. Similar-

For the club player to handle the pressure of an important match, he must regularly play matches which mean something.

ly in tennis, at the finish you must gather together your courage and mental strength and do what you are capable of and have trained yourself to do, calmly and deliberately.

Train yourself to become tournament tough. Just as it is useless for the matador to practice on a cardboard bull to lessen his fears of the bull ring, so there is no type of tennis practice that measures up to match play when it comes to the art of winning. You only learn how to win by getting out there and doing it when the chips are down. There is a certain hardening process that goes on during tournament play whereby players become less subject to the effects of fear and nerves. Without it, even the most experienced player will return to the circuit and, first time out, will choke like a novice.

Anything longer than a month away from the tour is enough to soften up the tough edge needed to acquire the winning habit. I was made painfully aware of this when I lost to Ray Moore in the Pacific Southwest Championships in 1970. At the time, I had been off the circuit for about a year and had not even played in local tournaments for some months. But I had been training hard, was in top physical shape, and assumed this was enough. As I discovered, it was not.

I led 5–4 in the first set and was suddenly overcome with the horror that I had absolutely no idea how to finish off the set. My nerves failed me completely. Instead of playing each point automatically, allowing instinctive reactions to take over as they do naturally when one is tournament tough, I started worrying and floundering around. Nothing came automatically and I had nothing to fall back on. I lost the first set and then collapsed completely.

The same process occurs at all levels. For the club player to handle the pressure of an important match, he must regularly play matches which mean something. He must become accustomed to the fears and anxieties which arise during the course of these

102

matches. Only then can he learn to control his body while under stress. This learning process, which is like any other learning process, takes practice.

Moreover, through a process known as "desensitization," these fearful emotions tend to decrease the more they are experienced. Psychololgists often use this process when they try to rid their patients of phobias. Take, for example, arachniphobia—the fear of spiders. First, the therapist puts his patient in a room where, at a distance, he can see a spider in a glass container. Then he moves the container nearer. The patient sees that nothing horrible happens and that he is quite safe. He moves the container onto the table at which the patient is sitting. Still nothing happens. Little by little, the patient learns to look without fear and, eventually and gradually, even to handle the spider. He has become "desensitized."

The same process works with emotions on a tennis court. If you have an important club tournament coming up, try to play some meaningful matches beforehand. Make a small bet or play for something to increase the pressure. Then the tournament will come as less of a shock to your psyche.

How to overcome the fear of choking. In my match with Ray Moore, I choked and choked badly. It was not the first time. Even when I was tournament tough, I choked on some occasions in close matches. These chokes did not cost me the matches, only some points. All top players choke sometimes. I have seen Ashe, Laver, Connors and even Borg do it badly. It does not usually cost them their matches. When it does cause problems for players, it is not the choke itself that is the problem, rather the *fear of the choke as a sign of personal weakness*.

A few years ago, I used to practice several times a week with a player who was close to me in shotmaking ability, but who rarely won. He had played college tennis for a major university, hit the ball well, but played low on the team and never beat anyone of note.

His problem was extreme personal insecurity. He had a violent temper which became more likely to flare the closer the match got. He was forever making excuses and finding reasons why things were not going his way. But the most interesting thing was his reaction to the point in our match at which he was in position to win. If, at this stage, he got nervous and missed a shot or two, he went wild. He became livid and berated himself in every conceivable way about being a choker and unable to win. From that stage on, he was finished, and yet it was not the choking itself that had finished him. It was his reaction to it—his fear of it. It was as if he had picked up a rock and seen a rattlesnake. His momentary attack of nerves had unleashed an underlying body of insecurity and fear which was completely out of proportion to the loss of a few points. One has to come to grips with the fact that everyone chokes at some time or another, even people like McEnroe and Evert. But the pros have the self-confidence to admit it to themselves and accept it as a normal human condition. They don't allow it to shake them. They just keep trying, knowing that if they do, their nerves will usually settle down and their muscles will relax. Sometimes they are wrong and they lose. That possibility is acceptable to the realistic and stable person.

I was not able to extricate myself from the nerves that collapsed my game against Ray Moore in that Pacific Southwest tournament. But the following week, I improved. A similar thing happened to Allan Stone in Manila.

In that particular match against Colin Dibley, Stone was caught in the web of fear that is spun for all of us whenever victory approaches. He might have been lucky and escaped. But Dibley is just the sort of guy to recognize that freedom, as Kris Kristofferson wrote, "is just another word for nothing left to lose." While Stone was trapped in his confusion, Dibley proceeded to prove that the right mental attitude wins tennis matches—even when you can barely walk.

CHAPTER 7.
SHATTERING YOUR OPPONENT'S MENTAL ARMOR

Most of the concepts we have explored so far have related to the problems which occur within one's own mind. But your opponent has his problems, too. Just as we have advanced some methods of minimizing our own troubles, here we will examine ways of magnifying his. For a distraught opponent will make winning that much easier.

There are a multitude of ways to win tennis matches. I have always envied guys like Jimmy Connors and Roscoe Tanner who are able to do it by blasting their opponents off court with the ferocity of their shots. But most of us have to rely on more mundane methods which, unfortunately, usually involve a lot of work. If you don't have heavy artillery, you have to outmaneuver the enemy and ultimately weaken his will to fight.

Anyone who has played tennis for any length of time knows that winning is a prolonged and often agonizing mental struggle. A close match may last for hours and to win it is necessary to concentrate with intensity from start to finish. Not only is that hard work, but it can be boring. At the same time, you are becoming increasingly hot, tired and physically uncomfortable. Maintaining resolve under these conditions is no easy task, but to win, you must. When your opponent's resolve dissipates, he is finished. Until that moment, he always has a chance.

However, unbeknown to you, your opponent is experiencing similar difficulties. I always found it hard to imagine that my opponent might be getting ready to fold when my own body ached with exhaustion, and a shower and a drink were starting to look better than the winner's trophy. Even though I knew intellectually that he must be as tired as I, my own pain had a certain reality that his could never quite match. But it's a little like poker: Sometimes you have to see just one more card. We will look here at ways of helping that card be a favorable one—of giving your opponent's mind a "nudge" that will increase your chances of victory.

Each player begins a match with a finite amount of mental reserves, just as he starts out with a limited amount of physical reserves. Many matches are won by physically exhausting one's opponent. You get into good shape, run around with him all afternoon and hope that he gets tired before you do. Solomon and Dibbs make pretty good livings this way. The rest of the pros also rely on it to some extent, depending on what other weapons they have. But few players realize that they must set out from the beginning of the match to drain their opponents mentally.

How do you go about this, since applying mental pressure is not as obvious as physical pressure? There are many methods and, if you are aware of the concept, you can improvise your own as dictated by the peculiarities of the match and the moment. The ultimate objective is to convince your opponent that he is going to lose. He must be worked into the state of mind where he emotionally feels it is hopeless to fight on. Top tournament players have tremendous mental resiliency. They are capable of struggling on for hour after hour, and the task of draining their mental reserves is extremely difficult. The average club player, on the other hand, has no such resiliency.

SLACKEN THE PACE

One powerful method is to take advantage of those times in the match when your opponent is under more mental pressure than you. At those times, slow down the pace of the match, so that he remains under this strain as long as possible. An ideal time to do this is when your opponent is leading and is eager to finish off the set or the match. As a general rule, the player who is ahead is under more pressure than the one who is behind. This may appear paradoxical, but is true nevertheless. The front-runner tends to become conservative and tries to hang onto his lead, knowing that if the match continues to progress as it has, he will walk off a winner. He may even begin to anticipate the sweetness of victory and savor the congratulations that are soon to be his. He does not want anything to change but subconsciously fears that it will. He suspects that the longer he stays out there, the more likely it is that something will go wrong. He does not want to wait for his prize any longer than he has to. He feels pressure because he is afraid you will wiggle loose. Slowing the match down will make him suffer. Keep him in the hot seat as long as possible. It will seem like an eternity to him.

I must distinguish carefully here between stalling and slowing down the pace of the match. I am not advocating the Nastase approach. He causes complete chaos, and people want to kill him. Rather, I am suggesting an almost subliminal tightening of the tongs around your opponent's forehead. Under no circumstances is the strategy to disobey the etiquette and morality of the game by standing around tying your shoes, stalling and starting a war with your opponent. But do take advantage of the fact that all players play at their own pace and are uncomfortable having to play at any other pace. Within the allowable time and rules you should proceed as slowly as possible. Your opponent should feel uncomfortable for a good long time, but not know why.

Let us analyze in detail what can happen if your

> **An ideal time to slow down the pace is when your opponent is leading and is eager to finish off the set or match.**

107

opponent gets ahead by a service break early in a set. I personally never really minded getting behind at this juncture. While, of course, I would have rather been ahead, I viewed this as an opportunity to work on my opponent's mind. First, I knew he would guard this service break jealously and sit on it like a mother hen, trying to hatch it into a set. He would work and concentrate very hard every time he served, lest his advantage slip away. At the same time, he would tend to lapse on my serve, making these games easy for me physically and mentally.

Hanging onto a service break for an entire set is an arduous task at the best of times. And it can be made more so. Make sure to walk slowly between points and take as much time as is reasonable between games. Take your time getting ready to serve or receive serve. Do not stall, just prepare yourself more deliberately than usual and make him sweat. The games will take a tremendous toll from him. If you should somehow manage to even the score late in the set, you will not just be even; you will be ahead. You will have had a relatively relaxed set mentally, since his major focus will have been on holding his own serve rather than breaking yours. Meanwhile, he will have expended tremendous mental energy trying to stay ahead of you. When the momentum changes, all this will have been for nothing. He will be demoralized and you will have every opportunity to quickly run out the set.

But even if you should lose the set, the extra strain on your opponent will pay dividends if the match lasts a long time. The human mind does not have endless capacity to withstand stress. An hour or two later, background noise, wind or a bad call will cause much more damage to his frayed nerves than it would have otherwise. It does not matter when he folds, only that he eventually does fold.

Finally, the slowdown may have an important benefit above and beyond draining your opponent mentally. When you are losing, any change in rhythm and pattern is to your advantage. If you allow the match to go along as smoothly as it is, you are likely to lose. If you slow down, you have a chance to gather yourself together and play better. By the same token, any change will disrupt your opponent's rhythm, alter the flow of the match and cause him to think. With any luck, he may start to worry, change his game, probably for the worse, and end up blowing his lead.

ASSAULT HIS SELF-IMAGE.
A second way to weaken your opponent mentally is to mount an assault on his self-image. In general, you must keep in mind that a person brings with him to the tennis court all of his "real" world psychological makeup. By better understanding some of the more important factors in this makeup, you can learn to use them to help win tennis matches. On or off the tennis court, our self-image is largely determined by feedback and information given to us by other people. They constantly react and thereby reveal what they think of us. These evaluations are, by and large, transmitted without words, and relate to our every ability and trait, both mental and physical. They are noted and weigh heavily in our own self-evaluations. Basically, what other people think of you, you think of yourself.

Suppose, for example, that people often appear uninterested when you talk. They may glance away during conversations, forget what you say or direct their conversations away from you when you are in a group. How would you react? You would probably be debilitated. You might conclude that you are dull or unattractive or both. But, in any case, if this went on for any length of time, you would be deeply affected. In fact, whatever the truth may be, we are trained to accept as reality the accumulation of other people's evaluations of us.

Similarly, on the tennis court, your opponent's self-image as a tennis player will be affected by your attitude toward him. If you fear him, he will feel

There are definite written and unwritten codes of behavior in tennis, but within these it is legitimate to try and debilitate your opponent in every way.

strong. If you disdain him, he will feel uncertain. If you respect him, he will feel confident. You must be careful, therefore, lest you supply your opponent with psychological ammunition to be used against you. Your objective is to undermine his confidence, and you mustn't forget it.

Again, let me emphasize that a tennis match is not exactly like a street fight. There are definite written and unwritten codes of behavior by which we must abide. But within these codes, it is absolutely legitimate to try and debilitate your opponent in every way. That is the object of the game. You cannot separate the mental and physical aspects. Making your opponent feel comfortable will make him play better and fight longer, whether you do it by massaging his ego or feeding him his favorite shots. An acceptable yet effective attitude is one in which you indicate to your opponent that you expect to beat him no matter what he does. Furthermore, you want him to feel that you have no fear of his game or abilities—that you are impervious to his finest efforts. By thus disdaining him, you make him feel weak. In convincing him of these things, the line that you must not cross is the one where you overtly attack° him by word or deed. Nastase often crosses the line by mocking, taunting or teasing his opponents. Connors sometimes goes overboard, too (although less and less as he matures), by making hostile gestures and the like at his opponents.

One useful technique is carefully to *avoid acknowledging in any way your own bad errors or good shots made by your opponent.* The objective is twofold: You do not want to let him know that you are hurt or let him see your vulnerability; and you do not want to compliment him. Compliments make him feel good, increase his confidence and help him play better. These are hardly consistent with your goals. In the ring, when a boxer gets hit in the mouth he doesn't say, "Nice punch." Why should a tennis player be expected to? An effective response to a great shot is simply to go about your business as if nothing had happened. Turn

110

around without looking up and walk, at your normal pace, into position to start the next point.

Cliff Richey was the master at this. We were close friends, yet when we played, I felt he didn't know I was alive. He never looked at me or spoke to me. He played at his own pace, which he refused to vary. He was nicknamed "the Bull," because he walked with his head down between points, had terrific determination and would run right over you if he got a chance. He would never quit, and when you played him, you could look forward to a long, unpleasant afternoon. The fact that you were facing an awfully tough man who didn't give two hoots about your poor efforts on the tennis court badly damaged your confidence.

Try compliments—with special effects. Cliff Drysdale and Manolo Santana used a different approach. They complimented their opponents in a tone that suggested condescension and the utmost confidence. Their carriage and demeanor were such that when they said "nice shot" you had the feeling that they had simply omitted saying "little man" at the end. Drysdale sometimes used to clap for his opponent's good shots on his racquet. However, he exuded such an irritating degree of confidence that Roy Emerson, the most placid of people, once threatened to wrap it around his neck if he persisted. Apparently, this approach does have its risks. Confidence, cockiness and condescension are sometimes hard to differentiate: while the first one is acceptable, the latter two may cost you friends. That confusion was the case at first with Drysdale. He ultimately became one of the most well-respected and best-liked players on the circuit.

This approach is not as different from the Richey approach as it might appear. Although one ignores his opponent while the other compliments him, both get the same message across: "Your best shots do not shake me or lessen my confidence in my victory."

In either of these approaches, it is important that

111

It is important that you do not let your opponent see your weaknesses. These encourage and strengthen him.

you do not let your opponent see *your* weaknesses. These encourage and strengthen him. They give him hope and keep him fighting longer. If you are tiring physically, hide it. If you miss an easy shot, do not cry out in anguish. He expects you to and it will shake him if you don't.

If you are nervous, don't broadcast it by rushing around, grousing at conditions beyond your control or telling people about it. I have actually heard players shout out loud, "I am choking!" What a tremendous psychological boost for their opponents! Everybody chokes. If you must choke, choke quietly. No matter what the circumstances, it is best to appear cool, deliberate and confident

According to H. S. Sullivan, the eminent neo-Freudian, we have powerful needs for security and approval from others, needs so pervasive that they often overshadow even our drive for physical satisfaction. If other people disapprove of us, we are intuitively aware of it and respond by becoming increasingly tense. According to Sullivan, we react by attempting to gain approval, thereby ridding ourselves of unpleasant and disturbing tension.

You can increase your opponent's tension by disapproving of him. Again, this disapproval must be transmitted in a covert and socially acceptable manner. If you are not careful, you will end up winning more tennis matches than friends and should be prepared to spend a lot of time with your trophies alone.

Here, again, the overall approach is to be businesslike. The pros provide the perfect examples. They are great friends off the court, but the routine banter and chat cease the minute they leave the locker room. If you have watched professional tennis matches, you may have noticed that the players barely recognize each other's existence while changing ends, much less indulge in friendly conversation.

As a non-professional player, your approach in a serious match should follow a similar pattern. It is not necessary to cut your opponent dead in the clubhouse. But, once out on court, don't laugh at his jokes, either. In fact, by your own businesslike and slightly aloof attitude, you can make it quite plain that you are not interested in his opinions, his jokes—or his best shots. You tend to your business and let him tend to his. Only when match point is over is it time for comments and congratulations.

All this should make him a little uneasy—assuming, of course, that he hasn't read this book first.

CHAPTER 8.
PSYCHING:
HOW TO DO IT,
HOW TO COUNTER IT

The scene could be any locker room on the pro tour. Erik van Dillen, the former U.S. Davis Cup player who stunned John McEnroe in the first round of Wimbledon in 1978, is picking up his gear after showering and heads for the door. His irrepressible humor bubbling just below the surface, van Dillen glances round, selects his victim and unleashes his parting shot.

"Don't listen to what everyone says about your volley, Tom," says van Dillen, barely able to keep a huge grin from spreading across his face, "I think it's terrific. It sure gives me a lot of trouble!"

With that he sweeps out, leaving Tom—be it Gorman, Gullikson, Okker or whoever—staring balefully after him, knowing full well it is a joke and, yet . . . . Isn't there always a grain of truth in humor? What had people been saying about his volley? Tom mentally runs through his last couple of matches. Maybe he did get passed a couple of times when he should have put the volley away. It starts to prey on his mind and there you have him—*psyched*.

"Of course, it's all done in fun but, psychologically, it's a brutal kind of humor," admits van Dillen, who is one of the most outrageous culprits on the tour.

114

There are, however, plenty of others.

The essence of a psych in something as instinctive as tennis is to make your opponent think. It is not important what he thinks about, just so long as he starts to think about something. Then the smooth coordination essential to proper shotmaking is disrupted. In addition, his concentration is distracted from the purposeful focusing on movement, patterns and stroking and shifts to the subject of the psych, whatever it may be.

Gardner Mulloy was a master at it. "Gee, your forehand's working well today," Mulloy would tell an opponent admiringly. Suddenly, the opponent would be conscious of his forehand, whereas before he had just been hitting it freely and instinctively. He might start to wonder if he could keep on hitting it as well and retain Mulloy's admiration. He might try to do even more with it to prove that this appreciation was well founded. Or, if he knew Mulloy and his reputation, he might ask himself, "Is Gar trying to psych me?" and this, too, would do some damage. In any case, disruption, distraction and deterioration would result.

Falling victim to a psych depends on several factors, but your level of intelligence is not necessarily one of them. Ray Moore, one of the brightest guys playing the game, proved it in the Australian Championships one year. Moore was playing the big, British left-hander, Roger Taylor, and, after a titanic struggle, led by two sets to love, 10–8, 12–10 (before tie breakers were used). Moore had won the second set with a drop volley, leaving Taylor exasperated in midcourt. "How can you be beating me?" he asked Moore with sarcasm in his voice. "You don't have any shots."

That was all it needed, because it blew Moore's mind. "I lost the third set 6–0," he recalled. "I just couldn't believe he had said that. All the way through the set I was thinking, 'Who is Roger Taylor, with the worst backhand in the world, to say that to me. Who does he think he is?' And, of course, while I'm think-

> The essence of a psych is to make your opponent think.

115

ing all that, I'm losing games by the minute."

Taylor and Moore were never the best of friends and Taylor knew exactly how to get through his opponent, regardless of his intelligence. He touched a nerve and let the indignation that erupted in Moore's mind do the rest.

Before we venture further into any analysis of a psych and how it works, I should point out that trying to psych your opponent just before or during a match is basically unfair play and is not being recommended here. Making a habit of psyching will invariably end your friendships with your fellow players. If you value these, you will use psychs sparingly. Moreover, there is the moral question. The victory, under these circumstances, just doesn't feel as good, although, admittedly, it is still better than losing.

However, since psyching does occur, understanding how it works may help you deal with this strangely effective piece of mental warfare. If someone is trying to psych you, it is possible to control the amount of damage it does because the effectiveness of a psych lies in the eye of the beholder. It will only work if you allow it to. Only when the recipient's mind already contains the seeds of doubt and fear will the aggressor be able to find fertile ground. Then, with a few well-placed words, he can make those seeds blossom into a fully fledged breakdown.

But if you are confident in your own abilities and disciplined in your concentration, no psych, regardless of its potential damage, can affect you.

FOCUS ON A WEAKNESS
As van Dillen has shown us, a common and effective variety of psych focuses on a weakness in some aspect of your opponent's game. Here the stage is set for insecurity because, if your opponent has a weakness, he will certainly know it. In the past, it probably would have cost him matches but now he prefers to forget about it. Picking it out and spotlighting it can make him feel distinctly uncomfortable.

116

A typical psych of this kind did some damage recently in an intercollegiate match at Pepperdine. Rocky Vazquez, one of my Pepperdine players, was struggling with an opponent who appeared to have a dodgy backhand. "Shots" Suresh, one of Rocky's teammates, was watching from the sideline. Occasionally, when the guy would miss a backhand, Suresh, under the guise of giving Vazquez encouragement, would shout, "That a way, Rocky! Keep coming in on that weak backhand." A little heavy-handed, maybe, but then college matches do get emotional, and Suresh was encouraged by the success his support was having as the visiting player's backhand deteriorated still further.

For a psych to work, it helps to know your opponent's weaknesses and how to probe them. Joking around in the locker room is one thing, but trying to mentally orchestrate an opponent's mind before a match is quite another. I am embarassed to admit that I did this in a match with Arthur Ashe when we were both at UCLA. Ashe and I were pitted against each other in an All Star match and I was going to have to play with a broken little finger strapped to the fourth finger of my racquet hand. Every time I hit certain shots it hurt, and I knew I would have to come up with some special ploy if I were to have a chance of winning.

So I searched around for some psychological ammunition to work with and decided I had two things going for me. Firstly, it was a nasty, windy day, dreary and overcast—the sort of day that would require a lot of motivation to get the average person out on court and even more to get him to battle through a long, tough match. Secondly, we were put out on court three where virtually no one would be watching, which further decreased motivation.

Ashe's personality is such that he likes to appear cool. He is not the Jimmy Connors or Cliff Richey type who is willing to scrape and scramble for every ball. This, of course, I knew and worked specifically on

For a psych to work, it helps to know your opponent's weaknesses and how to probe them.

117

decreasing his motivation to an absolute minimum.

"God! This is supposed to be a big match and they've got us stuck out here," I grumbled as we set off for the court. I continued in this vein and, when the warm-up started, I adopted a lackadaisical attitude and looked thoroughly disgusted and slaphappy about the whole thing. From all this, Ashe could only conclude that I considered the match unimportant and wasn't taking it seriously. So, naturally, he was not about to try if I wasn't going to try. At the time, Ashe hadn't realized that I *always* try. He got behind at the outset and could never quite gather himself together enough to stage a comeback. I won 6–3, 6–2.

ASSERT YOUR SUPERIORITY

John Newcombe used different methods to psych his opponents. He made himself unpopular with many players on the tour by continually asserting his superiority over them before matches. In a friendly, but quite serious, sort of way, Newcombe would start lecturing his opponent on some aspect of tennis or related subject so that, by the time they walked on court, the other player would be feeling intellectually inferior alongside this forceful, dominating champion. In that frame of mind, it didn't take more than a couple of intimidating volleys from Newk to make the victim feel physically inferior as well.

On the women's tour I have it on good authority that Virginia Wade psyched her opponents with similar tactics, although in a more haughty, distant way.

IMPERTURBABLE FOES

Sometimes attempted psychs backfire. Once I was playing Stan Smith in the finals of the Southern California Championships at the Los Angeles Tennis Club. As frequently happened, some well-lubricated members were making a terrible noise in the bar that overlooks one end of the center court. I was nervous and my nerves didn't need much distraction to fray them still further. To start with, Smith always drove me crazy. He was enormous, aggressive and never gave me a chance to play my own game. I was invariably frustrated. Secondly, he was always a perfect sport—imperturbable and never reacting in the slightest way whenever he missed a shot, no matter how easy. By some quirk, this made my sportsmanship and temper all the worse.

I figured that, as long as I was being irritated and bothered by the noise, I would make sure that Smith thought about the noise so that he could get irritated, too. So, as we changed ends, I said, in the sliest and most innocuous way I could, "How can anyone possibly play on that side of the court with all that racket?"

Smith looked at me in that quizzical way of his and said, "What noise? I hadn't noticed it." Then he walked serenely back to serve and continued to tear my game apart. That was the final straw. Smith, with his exceptional powers of concentration, had been able to block out the noise completely and even my clumsy attempt to force it into his consciousness had had no effect.

Among the women pros, no one dominated in quite the same way as Billie Jean King. Friendship with King off court became a liability whenever one faced her across the net, as Rosie Casals discovered to her cost on numerous occasions. Casals was a good enough player to have beaten King many times, but rarely did so. Her failure to clinch matches she should have won had little to do with technical ability and much to do with her inability to overcome King's extraordinarily powerful personality.

There was one occasion in the early 70's when Casals seemed to have the match under lock and key. She had been playing brilliantly and King, who was experimenting with a steel racquet at the time, was 4–0 down in the second set, having lost the first. At the end of that fourth game, King suddenly walked over to the umpire's chair, threw down her own racquet and picked up one of Casals' spares, asking her op-

> **Smith said, "What noise? I hadn't noticed it." My clumsy attempt to force it into his consciousness had failed.**

ponent if she could use it. As one of King's best friends, Casals could hardly do other than comply but, when the match resumed, she couldn't play tennis anymore. It was as if King had said, "Look, there's something wrong here. I'm the one who is supposed to be winning and yet you are leading 4–0 in the second set. It must be the racquet, so I'll just make a switch and everything will return to normal."

But, in fact, King did not have to say anything. Casals was so conditioned to the normality of her friend winning that just one simple, inconsequential act was sufficient to jar her confidence and bring her back into line.

Billie Jean King's overpowering personality was even too much for Bobby Riggs, the sneakiest psych artist of all time. When they played their famous "Battle of the Sexes" match at the Houston Astrodome, there was nothing the wily Riggs could do to get at King's mind because she was in her element. The greater the fanfare, the bigger the hoopla, the wilder the publicity, the better King liked it. To be a good candidate for a psych, one's mind has to be on the defensive and, particularly that night, there was nothing defensive about King.

Margaret Court, on the other hand, who had played Riggs in another male vs. female encounter a few months previously, was quite another matter and Riggs was well aware of it. Unlike King, Court was not at all comfortable with the circus-like atmosphere that surrounded the match. In addition, the Australian girl, shy and reserved by nature, may have felt she was carrying the pride and hopes of all women on her shoulders, and the responsibility made her feel even more nervous than usual.

Riggs realized all this and made the most of it. Before the match, small, slightly pot-bellied middle-aged Riggs, who even manages to *look* like a male chauvinist, if such a thing is possible, was running around giving interviews about how a woman's proper place is either in the kitchen or in bed. And, then, just before the match, he produces his master stroke. Grinning wickedly, he gives a little bow and presents Court with a bunch of flowers. What a timely, delicate little reminder that this *is* a battle of the sexes and that Margaret Court *is* a woman!

Confused by this unexpected display of chivalry, Court doesn't know whether Riggs is just trying to be nice or whether he is mocking her. Either way, he has achieved his main objective: He has thrown her off balance and made her think distractedly.

Basically, Riggs was much too smart psychologically for Margaret Court on that occasion but, eventually, he met his match at the Astrodome. There were no tender spots in Billie Jean King's aggressive, vise-like mind. Her self-confidence and disciplined concentration were an unbeatable combination. You should make it yours, too, if you want to be a winner.

Here is one last example of a psych, or a potential one, and how Yugoslav professional, Nikki Pilic, handles it. It is taken from "A Handful of Summers," a delightful autobiography by former touring player Gordon Forbes. Cliff Drysdale, Forbes' brother-in-law, is trying to provoke Pilic, his one-time doubles partner:

> "My dear Nikki," Cliff is saying in his provocative, light expansive way, "You must by now realize that your opinion of your game is higher than anybody else's. We all think you play at this level and you believe you play at *that* level."
>
> He uses his hands to demonstrate the difference in levels. They have been discussing recent defeats, victories, records. Cliff sits back with a bland, little smile as though only half his attention is required to verbally engage Pilic. Pilic's face is arranged into an expression of the profoundest disdain, his nose lifted as though Cliff represents a sewerage disposal works upwind from him.

"I have game for *any* level," says Pilic, "and also I can break eggs with volley!"

"Does that imply my volley cannot break eggs?" inquires Cliff.

"Not only eggs!" cries Pilic. He feels he is winning the exchange. "And not only volley. You have only one big shot!"

"And you, I suppose," says Cliff, "are blessed with a flawless game! What about that backhand that you have to dig out from behind you?"

John Newcombe, who has paused at the table and overheard Cliff's last remark, throws in an exploratory spanner.

"He's right, Nikki! You've got a terrible backhand. You couldn't pass your grandmother with that backhand!"

"Purpose is not to pass grandmother," says Nikki. "Purpose is to make good shot on big point."

And isn't that the purpose of all of this?

CHAPTER 9. THE PSYCHODYNAMICS OF DOUBLES

This chapter on doubles may sound like a chapter on marriage counseling. But, in a sense, a doubles partnership is like a marriage and should be treated as such. Many of the same dynamics apply.

The psychological problems one faces in doubles have everything to do with the complex interaction of differing personalities under situations of stress and excitement. Instead of the relatively straightforward one-on-one situation that occurs in singles, we are faced with having to cope with an intimate relationship with our partner while working on the possible destruction of the harmony that exists between our opponents. There are, therefore, four personalities interacting out there on court and that can really get complicated.

HOW TO BE SUCCESSFUL AS A TEAM

Should you and your partner be alike? In choosing a doubles partner, it is not necessary to find someone who is identical in outlook, taste and personality. You do not even have to be close friends off court, although that can help. But it is necessary to find someone whose habits and personality traits do not irritate you, because in moments of stress that irritation will be magnified until it looms as an insurmountable barrier to coexistence. Rather, you should try to select someone whose strengths and weaknesses complement your own. Harness whatever differences exist between you and make them work to produce a stronger, united front, both technically and psychologically.

John Newcombe and Tony Roche have formed what some people rate as the most successful doubles partnership of all time. Yet, apart from being Australian, there is little similarity in their backgrounds or personalities. Roche is a mildly introverted, typically easygoing, yet highly professional, Aussie. Newcombe is an extrovert, a natural leader, highly strung and dominating. Yet, in skill and tactical knowledge, there is little to choose between them, with Roche, if anything, holding the edge in natural ability.

This could have caused problems had not Roche readily accepted Newcombe's need to release nervous energy by talking and issuing instructions during a match. Frequently, Roche knew what Newcombe was going to say before he said it and sometimes did not necessarily agree with it. But he merely nodded sagely, letting the advice wash over him, thereby acting as a willing refuse dump for his partner's emotional overflow. It made Newk feel good and it was no skin off Roche's nose. Any sign of irritation on Roche's part would have dangerously threatened the team's mutually supportive balance.

Give your partner maximum support. The problem of self-confidence is enlarged in doubles play because a slump in one's own morale is not the only emotional result of a badly played shot. There is a feeling of guilt, too. We have let our partner down. Will he start to lose faith in us? Overall pressure in doubles may not be as great as it is in singles, but in moments of crisis it can reach an unbearable pitch if you are playing badly.

In doubles it is possible for your partner to be

124

carrying the whole load. Your team can have a set point before you, personally, have hit a ball in court. Try not feeling guilty about that.

The pressure can be extremely painful for the person playing the ad court. I remember one miserable occasion back in 1960 when Larry Nagler and I were playing Clif Mayne and Hugh Ditzler in the semifinals of the National Hardcourt Doubles Championships at La Jolla, Calif. Three or four times, Nagler got us to break point and each time I missed the crucial service return. I started to become paralyzed with fear and embarrassment. But he kept on winning the deuce point and I kept on failing to get the service return back over the net. It must have happened 10 times in that one game, and for the remainder of the match I was neither willing nor capable of doing anything other than pushing the ball back over the net and praying that Nagler would hit the winners. He did and we won. But one of the reasons why I didn't fall apart completely and drag Nagler down with me was the manner in which he reacted to my problems. Like any good partner, he was supportive and understanding.

And that spotlights the most important aspect of doubles psychology. At all times, give your partner maximum psychological support. The only way to do this is through sensitive and sympathetic channels of communication. *Never* lose sight of the fact that the overall objective is to communicate with your partner in such a way as to make him (or her) play his best. Make him feel good and the chances are he will play better.

But before you can communicate properly, you have to understand your partner's personality and make allowances for any individual quirks it may contain. Your reaction to those quirks must be calculated to increase his confidence and feelings of security.

Remember you and your partner are a unit— inseparable, indivisible. Neither can win without the other. Therefore, just as you try to put yourself in the best possible psychological state to win a singles

Never lose sight of the fact that the overall objective is to communicate with your partner in such a way as to make him play his best.

match, you must put yourself *and* your partner in the same state to win in doubles.

It is wise to remember that all of us crave the approval of our peers. The neo-Freudian psychologist Sullivan replaced Freud's emphasis on sex by making man's overwhelming need for approval the focal point of his thesis. He maintained that loss of approval from others caused anxiety and damage to one's self-image. In a high-stress, competitive situation, such as a tennis match, these feelings of rejection can be accentuated.

Unfortunately, it is an all too common occurrence for the better player to detach himself psychologically from a partner who is playing poorly. It is for protection of one's own ego. The worse your partner gets, the more you want to isolate him. It may reach the point where he feels you have almost joined your opponents on the other side of the net, suddenly making it a three-on-one situation.

This parallels the type of social situation at a party when your wife or husband says something stupid and you treat it as an affront to your own image. Normally, you look upon your spouse as part of yourself but now you want to disown him because he is making a fool of himself and you in the process. It hurts your ego, so you become embarrassed and unsupportive.

The same thing happens on a tennis court. There is an instinctive tendency to want to jump ship and let your partner sink by himself. You look to your opponents for sympathy and understanding and to show them it is not you who is losing the match. This conspiratorial understanding with your opponents makes your partner feel as if he has just caught the bubonic plague.

One sees this happening all too often in club tennis but rarely, if ever, on the pro tour. And with good reason. The pros know full well that unsupportive behavior and lack of good communication between partners is fatal to the team's chances of success.

So when your partner is playing badly, it is essential for him to know that he has your confidence and support. This can be transmitted to him in a number of ways, verbally or through gestures and expressions. Remind him of the times when he has carried the team, and when he does make a good shot, offer a special word of praise.

Pander to his idiosyncrasies and use whatever knowledge you have of his personality to bring out the best in him. It can be hard work, but remember you are working for yourself, too. No matter how disastrous the relationship may be, no divorce is possible until the match is over, so try to make the most of it.

Work as a unit. When we toured the world together as a doubles team in 1964–65, Donald Dell and I inevitably got to know each other inside out. By the time we had survived innumerable hazards—some physical but mostly emotional—over the course of a 12-month trip through Europe, Africa and Asia, lack of understanding was not our problem. But toward the end, we both let the tensions of the trip arrest the harmony of our doubles partnership.

On one occasion in Moscow, I was guilty of not following my own rule of working with my partner as a unit and accepting his problems as my problems. Whenever Dell got angry, nervous or frustrated on court his natural reaction was to lash out verbally at the nearest convenient targets, be they opponents, ball boys, officials or spectators. Usually, I tried to head off the worst of these scenes by talking with him and trying to calm him down.

We had made a special point of discussing the problem when we arrived in Moscow to play the Soviet National Championship. We had agreed that we wanted to be good representatives of our country in the Soviet Union. We certainly didn't want any "Ugly American" scenes in the shadow of the Kremlin.

But when our semifinal match against Colin Stubbs and Allan Stone got under way in front of a large crowd at Lenin Stadium, good intentions were quickly forgotten. After a tight struggle, we fell behind and sure enough Dell started berating the ball boys. I went crazy. I should have gone to his rescue, but instead I went into the tank, which is the tennis pros' term for throwing the match. With me not trying and Dell in a rage, we lost—just as we deserved to. I should have spoken to Dell and tried to correct the situation, but I was irritated and irrational. After all, what good does it do to lose the match? There is no point in sinking the boat when you are in it.

Avoid on-court banter. Dell and I tended to talk a lot when we played. Sometimes it was necessary and helpful. Often it was neither. As a general rule, you should be wary of too much talk during a doubles match. There is a great temptation to chatter away— especially if the pair of you are good friends and enjoy each other's humor. But this is distracting. It alters your focus and before you know it, you are paying more attention to entertaining your partner than winning the match.

Wojtek Fibak, who won the 1978 World Championship Tennis doubles title in Kansas City with Tom Okker, says that sometimes Okker's outrageous sense of humor leaves him doubled up with laughter at the net as the Dutchman is about to serve. Fibak finds that kind of easygoing relationship on court relaxing, but admits that it has to be kept in check, lest it begin to chip away at the team's concentration.

But, like Lee Trevino, who has an amazing ability to sink putts in the middle of a long, humorous dialogue with the crowd or his caddie, Fibak and Okker are very much the exception. For us less-gifted souls, I would strongly recommend that talk on court be kept to a minimum. It is too easy to allow chatter to become a substitute for play. There is a tendency to procrastinate and fantasize about what you are *going* to do, rather than getting on with the job of doing it. A tennis match is not a social occasion for the serious player and

128

too much talk tends to turn it into one.

Should you apologize for errors? Apologizing is an obvious, natural thing to do, particularly after missing an easy shot. But there are three main reasons why you should simply keep your lips closed and get on with the game:

1. Apologizing only highlights the mistake. In doubles, as in singles, you are much better off putting it straight out of your mind and concentrating on the next point.

2. Seeing you worry and verbalize about your errors only gives your opponents confidence and boosts their morale.

3. It is more likely that your partner will become upset with you because, by talking about the problem, it only confirms in his mind that you are, in fact, making a lot of mistakes. All of us have run into the whining, sniveling type who, instead of enlisting our sympathy, merely incites feelings of hostility. The more he whines and apologizes, the more you feel like kicking in his teeth. This cruel and somewhat irrational response to the sight of extreme weakness stems from the fact that it reminds us of our own inadequacies, which we fear and want to suppress.

Switch, rather than fight. Feelings of irritation toward your partner can also grow through the simple passage of time. As in marriage, you may become annoyed at your partner's weaknesses. It is not so much that your partner has a particular bad habit. Rather, it is the mind-numbing predictability of that habit surfacing under certain conditions which triggers the annoyance. On court, it can be the fact that he tends to lob short when he gets nervous. Or insists on poaching balls better left to you. The familiarity of these weaknesses make you cringe in anticipation and when, once again, your worst fears are realized, you become doubly frustrated and annoyed.

A fresh partner tends to be given the benefit of the

doubt and is generally treated more leniently in your mind. This is true in all walks of life.

When a company calls in an out-of-town expert as a consultant on some project, his advice is listened to with great deference. He is treated politely and is probably regarded with greater credibility than the in-house expert on the subject. There is a tendency to imagine he knows more than he does. But after a while, the sheen from this bright new brain begins to dim and you realize he is neither better nor worse than the guy still slogging away in the office next door.

It is wise to be aware of the staleness that can beset a doubles partnership. If you find that trivial things start to irritate and personality traits begin to have an adverse effect on the harmony of the relationship, it may be better to split up, if not permanently, then at least temporarily.

On the pro circuit, there are very few doubles players who stick to the same partner every week of the year. Often, it is simply that the problems of world-wide scheduling and personal commitments make it impossible for two players to compete in the same tournament week after week. But sometimes players deliberately take a break from each other—as Stan Smith and Bob Lutz did for a time—so as to resume with a fresh attitude and incentive.

Some players actively seek new partners on a more permanent basis. Okker, who now plays with Fibak, had a long-standing and highly successful rapport with Marty Riessen that stretched over a decade. Brian Gottfried, wishing to concentrate more on his singles, broke up his lucrative partnership with Raul Ramirez after the pair had won almost every important doubles title in the world.

But, with very few exceptions, these tennis divorces are arranged on a very amicable basis. The people concerned are pros and they know that, even though their relationship may not have been a love story, true professionalism, both on court and off, means never having to say you're sorry.

130

HOW TO TREAT THE OPPOSITION

So far, we have been concerned primarily with the problems arising out of having someone else on your own side of the net. But what about your opponents? Can you use your mind as well as your racquet to disrupt their partnership? Most certainly.

Exploit their weaknesses. If one of your opponents is weaker than the other, attack him immediately and at every reasonable opportunity. This will not only earn you points but, psychologically, it will drive a wedge between your opponents. By playing the weaker man, you will be publicly acknowledging that you have found the weak link in their armor and are intent on exploiting it. This will hurt the weaker man's confidence and make the better player feel he is being burdened.

You can play on this emotion by catching the eye of the stronger player whenever his partner makes a really bad mistake and, in a subtle, conspiratorial way, let him know that you sympathize with his position. Help to make him feel the weight of the albatross around his neck. If it gets too heavy, the chances are he will become so discouraged that he will no longer try as hard.

Intimidate them. It is also easier to intimidate your opponents in doubles than it is in singles because the net men are playing at close range. Yes, I am talking about physical intimidation, which is all part of the game—not the most genteel or attractive part, perhaps, but a legitimate strategy nonetheless.

Only on very rare occasions does it happen that you actually try to hit your opponent—that really is not part of the sport. But I think it is a definite advantage if you can make the other guy worry about his safety. In football, the minute a man starts thinking about getting hurt, he is finished. Although serious injury is virtually unheard of in tennis, everyone knows that a ball hit at a hundred miles an hour which connects between the eyes or in the groin will be excruciatingly painful. Without ever being hit, we know that such missiles are to be avoided at all costs. The sheer power of a shot hit at close quarters can serve as a reminder of this.

Instilling a little fear into our opponents certainly helped Donald Dell and I win one particular match during the course of our world tour. We were up against a couple of swift and cunning Italians in Florence. Both these guys were loose and cocky and were making fools of us with quick, angled volleys and fancy footwork on the red clay. The large Florentine crowd thought it was great sport and were baiting us at every opportunity.

That is not the sort of situation that appeals to Dell and I can't say I was enjoying it much either. But, with his naturally belligerent attitude toward adversity, Dell was not about to take it lying down. The first chance he got, he sprinted across the net and tried to ram an easy volley down the net man's throat. He hit the hell out of the ball and it whistled to within inches of the Italian's ear. Just to make sure the little chap knew what was happening, Dell stood there and snarled, "Next time, I'll take your goddamn head off!"

Suddenly all the looseness was gone. The Italians were paralyzed. No more fancy volleys and drop shots. From that moment on, they were more concerned with protecting life and limb than winning. We beat the hell out of them.

Physical intimidation can also make your opponents angry. As Pancho Gonzalez is about the only player who has ever performed better in a state of anger, this can also work to your advantage, although it is really not something I would recommend you attempt at club level. Winning is important, to be sure, but for most of us tennis is also a sport to be enjoyed by winners and losers alike (even if losing does hurt a bit).

However, enjoyment is not necessarily the object of the exercise when you have Americans and Russians on court in a tight match at Wimbledon. I remember one occasion some years ago when Dennis Ralston and Chuck McKinley were playing Tomas Lejus and Sergei Likhachev on Wimbledon's No. 1 Court. The Russians were a mean team and, after several near misses, Likhachev finally drilled Ralston with an easy volley. Ralston flipped out. He got so mad he spent the rest of the match trying to hit Likhachev and, of course, lost all his timing and concentration in the process. From a two-set-to-one lead, the Americans allowed the Russians to get right through them and lost.

But if trying to maim your opponents or stir them into a state of uncontrollable rage is not what tennis is all about in men's doubles, then it should certainly play no part in that more delicate and complex aspect of the game—mixed doubles.

INNUENDOS IN MIXED DOUBLES

Mix two men and two women together on a tennis court and the psychological possibilities are mind-boggling. In social tennis, the relationships between the players will influence each competitor's approach to the match. One can easily imagine that the attitudes of two husband-and-wife teams will be vastly different from those of dating unmarrieds. Winning the match may not be the primary objective.

But let us ignore specific interactions and assume that we have players who want to win, rather than play some variety of tennis charade for sexual purposes.

The basic winning attitude should be the same as in any tennis match—concentrate on attacking your opponent's weakness in any way you can, while keeping within generally accepted rules of court etiquette. This can put the male player in a squeeze. Assuming that both male and female players are of approximately the same standard, the man is usually physically stronger, faster and a better volleyer. This statement will, it's hoped, not be taken as a reflection of male chauvinism, rather one of physical fact. There are obvious skeletal, structural and hormonal differences that give males a physical advantage. The optimum winning strategy is for the female to play consistent, tactically sound tennis, while the male ferociously attacks the opposing female and intimidates her in every possible way. He should be mobile and intercept as many shots as possible. Hardly chivalrous, but effective.

There is a social limit to the vigor with which he may attack the opposing female. In trying to play the girl and yet not hit her between the eyes with easy overheads, he is prone to change his natural rhythm and miss simple shots or ease up too much and have her best him in the exchange. And he must be careful, lest he be so timid in his attack on the opposing female that his own partner is left vulnerable. After a ball or two whistles by her ear, she would be wise to encourage her partner to be more forceful.

On the other hand, if the man is simply not playing well or unable to perform the dominant role that is expected, his partner must be patient and supportive. As former American Wightman Cup player Julie Heldman pointed out to me, this is difficult because she is basically dependent upon him. He has the power and the ability to end points in a way that she cannot duplicate, no matter how well she plays. At these times, the female is subject to feelings of helplessness, anger or even jealousy of the opposing female because she has a partner who can do the job properly. It is like losing your queen in a chess game. Your opponent has a tremendous advantage in power and mobility. All you can do is scramble, cover up and feel helpless. But, unlike chess, where the queen does not generally return, in tennis the man can, at any time, come alive again, as long as team harmony and a positive attitude are maintained.

In addition, the contestants in mixed doubles matches are subject to the same mental pressures that accompany any match where strong and weak players are paired. The man must be mentally stable enough

134

to accept the possibility that his partner may not be his physical equal. Shows of displeasure will only upset his partner, make her tentative and cause her to play worse. He must guard against overplaying shots and trying to end points too quickly out of concern that his opponents will soon attack his partner. This can lead to a frantic atmosphere where the man takes wild gambles and his partner, feeling his lack of confidence in her, becomes intimidated into making the very errors he fears.

The female, meanwhile, is open to feelings of inferiority and embarrassment if she is being attacked or lobbed and cannot protect her side of the court. After a while, she may begin worrying more about upsetting her partner than she does about playing the game. However, women also have some potent psychological weapons at their disposal. In most male-female situations, the man is taught to believe that his natural role is one of dominance. He pictures himself as the bulwark of the team. The only potential challenge to his total court supremacy is the opposing male. The female can earn great psychological dividends if she is able, with any frequency, to best the opposing male in exchanges or to fool him by hitting down his alley as he moves to dominate the court. Once his confidence is up, he roams the court freely and can be most effective. But being out-played by his female opponent is embarrassing and hurts his confidence out of all proportion to the actual point damage. The thought that the opposing female has no fear of him and, in fact, feels that she can directly get the better of him, is frightening to most men. It will make them force their shots, restrict their movements and become generally ill at ease.

This is a very risky tactic and should be used with care. If it is not paying off, do not push it. Return to the basic strategy and hit to the man only for diversion.

CHAPTER 10. GETTING THE MOST FROM YOUR TEACHING PRO

FINDING THE RIGHT INSTRUCTOR

The major problem for someone searching for good tennis instruction is finding a well-qualified coach or tennis professional in whom you can place your trust. Unfortunately, tennis is still something of a black art. The game abounds with charlatans and people peddling their own pet theories. In many cases, advice from two tennis pros will be directly contradictory. It is a nasty position in which to find yourself after approaching both in a state of ignorance. If you knew enough to decide which was right, you probably wouldn't be taking lessons in the first place.

Although it might not be much consolation, it should be known that the problem is not restricted to beginners. Many of the top players in the world are equally confused by a myriad of conflicting advice when they suddenly develop trouble with their service swing or backhand. I wish there was an easy answer, but there isn't.

The same sort of thing happens in the medical area. I had a hip injury when I was in England some years ago and was treated by a leading British orthopedic surgeon. He told me to exercise it on a regular and rigorous basis. When I returned to Los Angeles, I visited another orthopedic specialist who is widely known for his work with professional football and baseball teams. He told me to rest it completely. When I heard that, I decided that orthopedic medicine was in need of more accurate research and did as I pleased. Countless players on the pro circuit have suffered similar fates.

Psychologically, it is absolutely essential to have faith in your teaching pro.

In tennis teaching, as in medicine, there is no simple formula that the layman can use to decide which expert is right. But in both areas, common sense applies. After all, the motions of the ball are determined by the basic laws of physics. If something your teaching professional tells you does not make sense, ask him why. Never be afraid to ask why things are done in a particular way. If you are left feeling uncomfortable by many of the answers, change teachers.

Even if your instructor is right, he is still no use to you if he cannot inspire your confidence. Psychologically, it is absolutely essential to have faith in him. Otherwise, you will not have the mental impetus required to grasp concepts and use them to progress. Without belief, you will tend to resist the advice being offered and will therefore never derive full value from the lesson.

From the standpoint of both pupil and teacher, credibility is essential. My friend, Larry Nagler, now a successful Los Angeles lawyer, tells me that he never goes into a lawsuit making ridiculous demands. He says that once you lose your credibility in one area of the case, the jury pictures you as untrustworthy and questions the validity of everything else you say. Similarly, the tennis professional must be careful and consistent in his statements. It is certainly reasonable to have an individualistic approach to teaching the game, as many instructors do, but the approach must be able to withstand logical scrutiny.

It is always wise to check the credentials of teachers before entrusting them with your game. Apart from the obvious great pros, such as Vic Braden, Tony Trabert, Bob Harman, Barbara Breit Gordon, Jean

137

Drysdale, Tommy Tucker, etc., selecting instructors who are members of the U.S. Professional Tennis Association, for which high standards are set, offers a reasonable degree of security.

STUDENT/INSTRUCTOR: A SPECIAL RELATIONSHIP

The student/instructor relationship over a period of time can become a close, personal experience. If the coach is knowledgeable and skilled in the art of imparting that knowledge, the relationship will produce psychological as well as technical benefits.

From the psychological standpoint, there is an effect similar to the transference effect in psychotherapy. Here the patient, or pupil, becomes very dependent upon the therapist or coach. The top-class teacher is seen as extremely knowledgeable and the pupil has a natural tendency to relinquish his own responsibility and simply "believe." This is quite a natural phenomenon, as recent exposés of the cultist mentality have dramatically demonstrated. It offers comfort and allows the pupil to pursue a course of action single-mindedly and free of doubt.

On the other hand, there is often a desire on the part of the pupil to fight the coach and test him—at least at the outset. In an attempt to bolster his ego, the pupil may try to play to his own strengths while covering up his weaknesses. While this will never fool a good instructor, it is a common charade and both sexes are equally guilty of it. But, of course, it is antagonistic to the whole concept of coaching. Why pay money just to have someone tell you how good you are?

The psychologists Otto Rank and Andras Angyal proposed interesting personality theories which relate directly to this problem. Although stated in differing terms, they agreed that human beings spend their lives trying to work out a compromise between their conflicting needs for individuality and surrender.

The world is filled with unknown perils. We know there are forces and situations that are far

138

beyond our own abilities to cope. As adults, we know our inadequacies only too well and can remember the times when we were children and had all-knowing, powerful parents upon whom we could completely rely. Regardless of whether they were good or bad, there was comfort in the fact that they were a known entity. The urge for surrender which exists in all of us is the desire to return, in some measure, to this dependent state.

Individuality occurs in the various separations and personal readjustments that each of us undergoes, such as birth, weaning and leaving home to seek one's own place in life. However, this process can become fearful as we find it necessary to take on greater and greater responsibility and become increasingly alone and lonely in the process. Yielding to the simultaneous urge for surrender calms these fears. In giving up individual decision-making and responsibility, we attempt to become a part of something greater than ourselves. This would be typical of the "company man," the civil servant or church member. Yet, often people do not fit those labels quite so neatly and vacillate between the opposing forces, trying to reach a compromise that best satisfies their personal needs.

In the case of the coach-pupil relationship, this conflict is often resolved when the coach finally convinces his students that he has superior knowledge. After that happens, the pupil usually surrenders completely and begins to accept the words of the coach as gospel. In extreme cases, I have seen numerous young players believe so strongly in the teachings of their mentors that any attempt to change their strokes causes disturbing emotional reactions.

CHAPTER 11. AVOIDING PSYCHOLOGICAL PITFALLS

One of the first things a trainee pilot learns in stormy weather is not to get taken in by those spaces that appear in the clouds—sucker holes, we call them. They beckon you on temptingly when you should turn back.

It is a pity tennis players don't learn as fast as pilots when injured, for weary opponents offer up the same kind of sucker holes on their side of the court. I have often seen players change a winning game to try and take advantage of an opponent who is tiring or suffering from some small injury. They are not content to play their normal games. They want a sure victory so they pounce eagerly on what looks like an easy opening. It is often not as easy as they anticipate.

What usually happens? The player who has been sucked into switching tactics must now hit shots with which he is not familiar. With his normal patterns cast aside, he often ends up losing his rhythm, timing and maybe the match.

He would have done better had he stayed on course and continued to play the way he does normally. In most circumstances, it is very unwise to suddenly start doing something differently just because your opponent gets injured or tired.

140

Let us look in detail at various things that can happen when either you or your opponent is handicapped by fatigue, injury or aging—for the last of these is basically no different from the others. Aging is a case of gradual injury that doesn't heal. Not a pleasant way of looking at it perhaps, but true.

FATIGUE

When your opponent is tired. Anyone who has been in a long, tough match knows what a reassuring moment it is when you suddenly realize the person on the other side of the net is in even worse shape than you are. He starts to puff, his step in between points has lost its spring, and once the ball is in play, he is not covering the court as well. "Good," you think to yourself, "I've got him. He's not going to be able to last much longer. All I have to do is work him, make him run and not make any mistakes."

It sounds like a terrific plan. But it isn't. Because in your anxiety not to make mistakes, you change your game and become tentative. Instead of going for the sidelines and taking your chances, you start hitting down the middle. Instead of running him more, you end up running him less. Instead of approaching the net on his short shots and going for the kill, there is the temptation to hang back and work him over. The need to make him run becomes almost an obsession, so you try drop shots and lobs—anything to sap his strength. But few players can suddenly start hitting drop shots to perfection. The chances are you will net a few or hit some too long so that he is able to get back some points you should have finished off.

Convincing yourself that this is all right because you are tiring him out in the process is dangerous thinking. Whether or not he is becoming exhausted, one thing that is certain is that you are wrecking your rhythm. Later on, if your opponent doesn't oblige by collapsing when you want him to, you may not be able to recover that rhythm when you need it.

But quite apart from the physical result of any

141

change in strategy, it is a bad psychological ploy to alter your game at this stage.

Tiredness is partly mental. If you are playing a tough match and have the upper hand, your opponent will be more tired than when he has the advantage. There is nothing more exhausting than scrambling for ball after ball and losing the points. If a player sees no weakness in his opponent's armor, fatigue seems to descend with undue haste. Give him an opening and it may evaporate. Moreover, toward the end of a match the psychology of a tired person is that of someone who has nothing to lose.

As the will of an exhausted player drains away, the possibility of defeat becomes probability. And once he accepts that probability the pressure is off. He starts to feel relaxed. Everything seems just that little bit easier. The tension starts to ease and he doesn't feel so bad. And if, on top of all that, you suddenly switch tactics and become very conservative, your opponent will glimpse the first ray of daylight he has seen in a set or more. Every time he scrambles out of a point you should have nailed, his morale improves. If you fail to finish him off, if the knockout punch he has been expecting never comes, he may just start feeling pretty good again—good enough to come back and win. So why change? It was your normal game that got him tired in the first place—apparently you were running him enough then. So stick to it.

When you are tired. I used to approach this problem in two quite opposite ways, depending on the circumstances:

1.) *Never let my opponent see I was tired.* I would try to hide my fatigue as best I could whenever I was playing a big-hitting, confident serve-and-volley player on cement or grass. Why? Because the chances were he was not going to change his game whether I lived or died. With a style like that on a surface like that, his options were virtually non-existent. He *had* to play like that—often because it was the only way he knew how. I used to concentrate on trying to act as normally as my condition would allow and always kept my back to him when we changed ends. That way he could not get a close look at any tell-tale signs of fatigue on my face. I did not want to give him any encouragement, just in case he was also feeling weak.

It was like those contests we used to have as kids to see who could hold his breath longest under water. If only you could have known exactly when the other kid would bob to the surface, you could probably have managed to hold your breath for the few extra seconds necessary to win. On court the same principle applies. If an opponent can detect when your air is about to run out, he may manage to hang on just long enough to outlast you.

2.) *Let him see my fatigue and perhaps even exaggerate it.* I would try this when I knew I had enough stamina to go on and when I felt that my opponent was not a very confident type who might be tempted to change his game. If I could sucker him into being more conservative, it would suit me fine, give me more time to breathe. So I would huff and puff, let my shoulders droop and walk around real slow. It was a great act. As an added bonus, the crowd tended to come around to my side under those circumstances, and I actually felt quite the hero on a number of occasions—battling doggedly against the twin foes of a tough opponent and physical exhaustion. But no matter how exhausted I looked I nearly always had some reserve strength left, and often my opponent didn't look so tough after he had switched tactics prematurely to hasten my demise.

The late Rafe Osuna of Mexico was a master of these tactics. In the Interzone Davis Cup tie against the United States at Mexico City in 1962, Osuna faced tough Jack Douglas in the crucial fifth match with the score tied at two rubbers each. Osuna had been playing away from Mexico in the preceding weeks and was

**Fatigue is often
psychological—the loser
always feels more tired
than the winner—and the
more secure you feel
about your own fitness,
the easier it is to deal with
tiredness when it arrives.**

not acclimatized to the 6,000-foot altitude. Of course, neither was Douglas but, as an ex-football star at Stanford, he was as strong as a horse. Osuna, on the other hand, always looked weak—usually deceptively so.

Although Osuna took an early lead, Douglas fought back and leveled the score at two sets all. By now, Osuna was rolling his eyes to the heavens and flopping down in his chair between games, sucking oxygen. Douglas relaxed and it proved fatal. To the ultimate glee of 8,000 wildly partisan Mexicans, Osuna raised himself from the ranks of the near dead to run out the fifth set and then collapse tearfully into the arms of his countrymen. Douglas returned to the United States dejected and disgusted with his performance. He never competed internationally again and was forced to console himself by making several million dollars selling real estate in California.

Ken Rosewall is another wily pro who can never be counted on to be as tired as he looks. Anyone who watched that classic WCT final of his against Rod Laver in Dallas will never forget how exhausted little Kenny appeared in the fifth set tie breaker. He wasn't doing it to fool as experienced an opponent as Laver, of course; he probably was pretty tired. But he only looked it *between* points. With Laver ahead and serving to finish off the match, Rosewall moved like lightning the instant the ball was in play. He rammed two backhand service returns down Rocket's throat and served out the last point to win the match in a flurry of razor-sharp tennis. If Rosewall was indeed a weary man, it did Laver no good.

Until my senior year at college, I was always troubled by tiredness, even though I practiced long hours and kept in shape. But it was only in matches that I seemed to get tired, which was one of the main reasons why, in those days, I was a much better practice player than match player.

Then, in 1961, I started to run every day. No one told me how far I should run so I used to go off on my own and complete about a mile. That, for an athlete, is

144

not a great distance and bears little relation to the kind of stamina required to last through five-set matches without tie breakers.

But, whether or not my little mile run was helpful physically, it was an enormous boost psychologically. I won many more matches shortly after I started running. I had become convinced that I was stronger than my opponent, that I could outlast him if it came to a question of endurance. This belief gave me the will to fight on where previously I would have folded. It made me realize that I had a far greater reserve of physical energy than I thought. And, certainly, this is true of everyone. Just as we do not use all the brain power nature made available to us, so we rarely use all the physical resources at our disposal. As we have noted, fatigue is often psychological—the loser always feels more tired than the winner—and the more secure you feel about your own fitness, the easier it is to deal with tiredness when it arrives.

Many players during their years of peak physical condition surprise themselves by what they can achieve under what might be described as adverse conditions. At a tournament in St. Petersburg, Fla., for example, I went on an all-night binge after beating Jaime Fillol, then a young student at Miami University, in the semifinal. It was a fun celebration, but hardly the right preparation for meeting the talented Yugoslav, Nikki Pilic, in the final. I remember staggering back to my hotel with the dawn and sleeping until half an hour before match time. I was dead tired after hitting the first couple of balls. But I stalled as much as I could, played at my own pace, hung in there, and eventually Pilic got tired and quit in the fifth set. If he only knew! But it was also because I had a basic confidence in my overall condition that I was able to force myself to keep going that long.

COPING WITH INJURIES
When you are suffering from some kind of physical debility, it is possible to experience a sudden switch in

pressure. From being quite relaxed—a normal state when you feel you have absolutely no chance of victory—you can suddenly come under intense pressure, if you manage to work yourself into a winning position. For once there, you know it is a question of now or never. Your condition is not going to allow you to come back a second time, so the chance to serve for the match or reach match point carries with it a very special kind of desperate tension.

In an early-round match against John Alexander at the 1968 French Championships, my problem was a meal I had had the night before with another Aussie, Bob Carmichael. We had found a little Alsatian restaurant serving what seemed to be delicious knockwurst and sauerkraut. Unfortunately, it wasn't as good as it looked. While Carmichael's stomach, like its master's voice, had merely growled ("Yeah, mate, felt a bit of a twinge—nothing too serious, though") mine had rebelled. I was up all night and when I walked on court with nothing inside me except tea and a piece of dry toast, I was hardly in terrific condition to go five sets on slow European clay.

But by the time the fifth set duly arrived four and a half hours later, I was in really bad shape. I had started cramping and I didn't dare take salt pills with my dodgy stomach. However, I struggled on and got to 6–5, 30–15 on my serve. Until then, I had been careful not to do anything extravagant physically so as to keep the cramps at bay.

But on the next point, I came to net behind my serve and Alexander hit a backhand return which hit the tape, bounced up and hung there—the sitter of all sitters. I got so excited at the prospect of two match points that, instead of placing it carefully out of his reach, I leaped up and nailed it as hard as I could. As I hit it I felt every muscle in my body seize up. I went down in a knot of pain. There I was in the ridiculous position of having two match points and not being able to stand up to play them.

Harry Hopman, the great Australian Davis Cup

coach who was looking after Alexander at the time, was very sporting and told Alexander to give me some time to recover. It took me about five minutes and when I managed to get back into the serving position, I knew I had about four shots left in me—four shots to finish the match. More than that and I was sure to go down again. I pooped in a serve and Alexander, who was as petrified as I, pushed back a little ball down the middle and charged the net. "Great!" I thought, "that's just where I want him." But, again, I got too excited and hit the intended passing shot way out. I wouldn't make that mistake again, so I made a different one. On the second match point, I immediately came hobbling into the net myself. The coward lobbed me! I couldn't jump and that was it. Deuce and I quit. The pressure of knowing I had to win one of those two points had been too much. I defaulted and vowed never to eat sauerkraut in France again.

> My guideline for determining whether to rest an injury or play on it is: Play on it and, if it gets worse, quit!

Use your common sense. The most debilitating psychological factor one faces with injury is not the pain itself, but the fear that playing with the injury will cause further damage. Generally, severe pain serves a purpose. It is a warning signal that damage is occurring to certain parts of the body and that protective measures need to be taken.

But most tennis injuries are less than severe. Slightly torn or pulled muscles and tendons cause discomfort. But providing you do not have to grit your teeth in pain, it is usually all right to play. If you can compensate in some way so that the injury is not taking full stress, you are unlikely to damage yourself further. My usual guideline for determining whether to rest an injury or play on it is very complex and scientific: Play on it and, if it gets worse, quit!

The latest party line among sports medicine practitioners is that an injury should be iced regularly and rested for the first 24 to 48 hours after the injury occurs. On the assumption that tissue has been torn, this will allow coagulation and decrease fluid seepage and swelling. After that, heat treatment and "reasonable" exercise should begin so as to increase blood circulation and promote healing.

The word "reasonable," of course, is vague and open to a variety of interpretations. Unfortunately, orthopedic medicine is not yet the advanced science we would like it to be. All too often, we are forced to live with ambiguity. So be prepared to use a good measure of your own intuition and common sense in dealing with minor injuries. You should certainly seek the advice of a doctor or trainer if you are in any way unsure or unfamiliar with the type of injury you have received. He may not be able to do much, but an expert opinion may at least ease your mind.

One of the few physical benefits of growing older is that you get to know your body better. You learn which injuries heal quickly, which don't and what the pain signals mean. No coach, trainer or doctor can tell precisely how much your particular injury hurts or precisely when it hurts. The only absolutely true monitoring device for pain lies in the brain of the sufferer. The sooner you are able to read the signals correctly and match them up with past experience, the sooner you will be able to look after your own body properly.

Playing with pain is the norm. Despite all the assistance that is available to them (many top trainers now travel regularly on the world circuit), the pros quickly become experts at reading their own body signals. At most tournaments on the pro tour, prematch rituals in the locker rooms include a vast array of liniment applications, tapings, strappings and rubdowns by the trainer. Few pros walk on court totally free from injury or pain.

Todd Fullerton, who travels the international circuit full time as the ATP trainer, knows better than anyone just what kind of physical problems the players carry on court with them. Says Fullerton, "I would say no more than five percent of players on the tour are totally free of injury, but with the help of a

148

taping or a rub they just get out on court and learn to live with it."

Playing with injury is not much fun, but it is accepted as part of life in competitive athletics. Tom Gorman and Dick Stockton have chronic back injuries and rarely play without wearing full back corsets. Despite his numerous title-winning achievements, former U.S. Open Champion Manolo Orantes has rarely managed a 12-month period free of quite serious knee, elbow or back problems during the past six years. Bob Lutz has had both knees operated on, as has Billie Jean King. Evonne Goolagong's speed was hampered by a damaged Achilles tendon during much of 1978 and surgery was contemplated. Stan Smith and Tony Roche have had terrible elbow problems (as have most pros at one time or another, although less severely) and Arthur Ashe limped his way around the circuit for years, winning hundreds of thousands of dollars annually, before the bone spur on his heel finally forced him to the operating table.

Once the pros have been badly injured, they are usually never the same again, even though the injury may heal. The pain and fear leave psychological scars. Never again do they play with quite the same abandon. Always lurking in the back of their minds is the thought that, if they push too hard, the injury might recur.

Before he developed an elbow injury in 1973, Stan Smith had dominated American tennis for five years. In 1974 he dropped out of the top 10 rankings and, even though his elbow recovered, he never recaptured the towering force and dominance that caused Ilie Nastase to nickname him "Godzilla" back in the days of their arch-rivalry in the early 70's. Typically, Smith spoke so seldom about his elbow problem that few people realized how serious it was. However, he has admitted that the injury has somehow shaken his confidence.

> **Once the pros have been badly injured, never again do they play with quite the same abandon.**

How to use injuries to advantage. Before we get too gloomy about the inevitable wear and tear of our bodies, let us look at the positive side of injury because there really is one. Obviously, it only involves relatively minor injuries but, nonetheless, once you have decided you are fit enough to play, it is sometimes possible to turn injury to your advantage.

Marty Riessen won the Rothmans International at London's Royal Albert Hall one year with a string of upset victories despite a nagging arm injury. Riessen said later, "Somehow the injury helped me mentally. It took my mind off the pressures of the match." Injury can offer a psychological refuge from pressure. It is a built-in excuse, at least in the early stages of the match. You are not expected to win, so you can hit with abandon.

Although Riessen was successful despite his arm injury, leg injuries are usually overcome more easily. Even without his normal mobility, a player who is hitting the ball exceptionally well is capable of getting his opponent into serious difficulties. It is not necessary for him to run much. In both men's and women's tennis, I have often seen the injured player's shots become so severe that they take control of the match. The only problem occurs when he actually gets into a position to win the match. Then the pressure can reassert itself.

I ran into this problem, against a fully fit Marty Riessen in the semifinal of the Pacific Southwest Championships in 1967 when I was defending champion. My normal style is to scramble and maneuver my opponent out of position. But in an earlier match, I had strained a calf muscle and was unable to push off with my left foot. So with no options and nothing to lose, I started out the match by putting more on the ball. I was connecting well and surprisingly won the first set and kept it even until late in the second. At that stage, it suddenly dawned on me that I could win the match. Instinctively, I stepped on the brakes and slipped back toward my customary conservative style.

150

But, of course, I was not able to move as well as usual. Riessen eventually pulled out the second and third sets, 7–5, 7–5, but the fans thought I had played a great match.

In general, when a player reaches a crucial stage of a match he will employ tactics that are most familiar to him. There are certain weapons that have served him well in the past and he automatically relies on these in times of stress. In my case, I tended to hit conservative shots when things got tight and depended mainly on my speed to win points. In the crunch, I always felt uncomfortable going for winning shots and this trait proved my undoing in the Riessen match.

The lesson here is that if you are effective in changing your style to accommodate an injury, beware of lapsing back into old habits when you get into a position to win the match. Remind yourself of why you have been playing that way. It was because you were physically incapable of playing your normal game. So reverting to it at the most crucial point of the match simply is not going to work.

ADAPTING YOUR GAME TO YOUR AGE

For the athlete, the major problem in aging is the progressive loss of function due to injuries which do not heal. Naturally this affects our physical prowess, but it is doubly destructive because of the damage it does to our psyches. When a professional athlete ages and loses the quickness the public has come to expect, people say, "His legs are gone," or, "She can't run like she used to," and they believe, somehow, that the leg muscles have simply lost their ability to flex like a young person's.

But, most often, it is merely that a knee hurts here, a heel hurts there and a tendon is sore somewhere else, making certain movements painful. The athlete does not *want* to push for that extra burst of speed for fear of getting hurt. There is an increased awareness of the ever-present possibility of further

151

The greatest psychological obstacle to overcome is the sudden and often shocking realization that you can no longer play the way you used to.

injury—there are, after all, painful little reminders of that possibility being transmitted from various parts of the body. They no longer play with abandon.

The greatest psychological obstacle to overcome is the sudden and often shocking realization that you can no longer play the way you used to and that the ability to do so will never return. When I was in my early 20's I used to run violently after every ball. No matter what the score, I figured that if I got just one extra ball back, it would eventually increase the pressure on my opponents. They would try to hit wider and deeper to get away from me and, sooner or later, they would miss.

But, in my late 20's, the injuries started. Little by little, I found myself unable or unwilling to make the desperation lunges for the ball that had been the hallmark of my game. I was temporarily nonplussed. At first, with my primary weapon taken away, I didn't know what to do to win. When I needed a point and couldn't revert to scrambling, I became nervous. Under pressure, a player usually reacts best by carrying out habitual, unthinking patterns. Once he is forced to change and think, the door to unstable and nervous emotions is unlocked.

Pancho Segura once said, "The first thing to go is your eyes. The second is your nerves." With the loss of youthful abandon comes an increase in conservatism and fear. To some extent, of course, this is true in all walks of life, but golf, a less physically demanding game than tennis, provides an interesting example. In their later years, Ben Hogan and Arnold Palmer apparently continued to hit the ball as well as ever off the tee but developed what golfers call "yips" in their putting. This is similar to a hitch in the stroke and has little to do with any physical disability. It is caused by nerves.

But what causes this increase in nervous tension? One man who knows all about the problems created by a lifetime in competitive sports is former Wimbledon champion Jack Kramer, who owns a golf course

152

near Los Angeles and has studied the game over a number of years. Jack feels this condition is derived from "accumulative pressure," or the tension that has built up after years of competing. This is a popular viewpoint, but one with which I disagree.

No matter how imperceptibly, everyone suffers some kind of physical loss as they move into their middle years. It may be small but nevertheless forces fractional changes in habit patterns. The golfer may swing with his usual energy off the tee but find that the ball is carrying slightly less than usual. Or, due to a slight decline in visual acuity, the chip may not be quite as precise as before.

The golfer starts to compensate by making minor adjustments in old habit patterns. This coincides with the loss of his blind confidence in his former ability. It is this loss of confidence that becomes the real problem and it is this which carries over to the putting green.

To understand what the feeling is like, picture the problems facing older people when their senses become less acute. The degree may vary, but the effect is similar. As hearing and vision decline, there is a gradual increase in the number of nasty surprises elderly people have to face—a near miss by a car while crossing the street, a bent fender while driving or a bad fall. After a while, they start moving very cautiously, not simply because muscles and joints become stiffer, but because they are wary of everyday experiences they no longer seem able to control. Confidence and reliance in old habit patterns begin to erode. They become afraid.

Contrast this with the carefree experimentation of youth. As a youngster, your physical powers are always on the increase. You are on the upslope and, until it is reached, you have no real idea of where the plateau lies. Emotionally, you feel capable of anything. In theory, no task is too difficult for your developing powers. If not now, you think, then certainly some day your ambitions will be realized.

Maturity is reached when your emotions, thinking processes and reality itself coincide.

The key to contentment: accepting reality. Once your powers level out or even decline, you acquire an entirely new emotional outlook. Reality has struck. Often it happens without conscious realization. Maturity is reached when one's emotions, thinking processes and reality itself coincide.

But you've got real problems when your conscious mind tells you one thing, your emotions tell you another and reality is different from them both. This is the case with the older player who constantly looks backward and feels emotionally cheated because he can no longer make the shots and moves he once did.

How does one deal with this problem? By realistically understanding and accepting your own strengths and weaknesses. And that means your strengths as they stand right now, not as they were or will be. Only then will you be truly effective and in harmony with your age.

Sven Davidson, the former Swedish champion who is now a leading member of the Grand Masters tour, is a fine example of a player who has come to terms with the passing years.

"I don't find it frustrating," Sven revealed. "I enjoy playing just as much as I ever did. Of course, there are things you have to adjust to. I can't see under lights as well as I used to and none of us can hit the ball as penetratingly as we did before. But that's all right, because we are not competing against Connors or Borg; we are playing against ourselves. I don't worry about the fact that the Sven Davidson of 1979 wouldn't get a game off the Sven Davidson of 1957. It has no relevance."

In summary, new methods of play and tennis weapons must be developed to replace those that are no longer functional. The most difficult stages are the transitional periods during which an important ability has been lost and there has been insufficient time to develop new understanding and strategy to fill the gap. But don't be discouraged. It is common to suffer from unexpected bouts of nerves at these times. With

154

understanding, they can gradually be brought under control.

The great Roman thinker Cicero once said, "At my age, I don't yearn for the physical vigor of a young man any more than in my youth I yearned for the vigor of a bull or an elephant. Use what you have; that is the right way. Do what's to be done in proportion as you have the strength for it."

Follow that advice and perhaps you will be able to turn the shadows of autumn into the sunshine of Indian summer.